Mind
Over Money

Psychology Hacks for Winning Salary Talks

By
Sasha M. Greene

i

Mind
Over Money

Psychology Hacks for Winning Salary Talks

Table of Contents

Introduction

In the modern professional world, salary negotiation is not merely a transactional exchange but rather a critical skill that can determine one's career trajectory and financial well-being. It's a blend of art and science, requiring a fine balance of assertiveness, strategy, and understanding of human psychology. Yet, many people shy away from it, either due to lack of confidence or fear of confrontation. This book aims to dismantle those fears and empower individuals to approach negotiations with knowledge and tact.

We live in an era where the job market is becoming increasingly competitive, and knowing how to negotiate effectively can be the difference between settling for less and reaching your full potential. Salary negotiation is a vital tool for professionals at all levels—from those just starting their careers, to mid-level managers looking to climb the corporate ladder, and even seasoned executives seeking to maximize their value. By mastering negotiation skills, individuals can not only improve their financial outcomes but also gain deeper respect and recognition in their professional settings.

The framework of this book is designed to provide a comprehensive roadmap to successful salary negotiations. It's structured to guide you from understanding the psychological underpinnings of negotiation, through the practical steps needed to prepare and execute a successful discussion. The process is iterative and dynamic, just like the career paths of those who undertake it. Each chapter delves into critical aspects that contribute to effective

1

negotiation, ensuring you're well-equipped at every phase of the conversation.

Delving into the realm of negotiation requires overcoming mental barriers and societal expectations that often discourage self-advocacy, especially when it comes to financial discussions. This text will explore various psychological strategies that have been proven to bolster negotiation success. From addressing deep-seated financial fears and challenging traditional money mindsets, to harnessing the power of anchoring and reciprocity, these principles can radically transform your approach and outcomes.

One of the most challenging aspects of salary negotiations is building the confidence to assert your worth. The fear of rejection or the anxiety of confrontation can be overwhelming. However, confidence is not an inherent trait but a skill that can be nurtured and developed. Through role-playing scenarios and practical exercises, this book provides the tools necessary to foster a strong, confident negotiating persona. In doing so, you'll discover how to convey your value effectively while maintaining a collaborative and positive tone.

Timing and strategy are crucial elements that dictate the flow and success of any negotiation. This book will illuminate the significance of discerning the right moments to negotiate, whether during job offers or performance reviews. Crafting a strategic plan tailored to each negotiation's context can significantly enhance your bargaining power. Additionally, communicating effectively is paramount. Understanding verbal cues and the art of active listening can dramatically shift the negotiation in your favor. Learning to articulate your case succinctly and powerfully will make a compelling impact.

Navigating employer tactics, especially lowball offers, necessitates a well-rounded understanding of negotiation dynamics. This book arms you with counterstrategies to ensure you secure a fair remuneration. Recognizing and responding to these tactics with grace turns potential roadblocks into steppingstones toward achieving your salary goals. Furthermore, anyone taking the negotiation journey must be prepared to handle rejection. Resilience and perspective transform a declined request into a future opportunity for advancement.

The journey through this book is not just about the financial benefits; it's also about personal growth. Enhancing your emotional intelligence, understanding cultural nuances in negotiations, and leveraging technological advances are pivotal skills in today's interconnected workplace. Whether you're navigating a remote negotiation environment or dealing with multi-cultural teams, adaptability and awareness are key attributes to refine.

Importantly, this book addresses gender and cultural considerations, exploring how these factors influence negotiation dynamics. Recognizing and overcoming gender biases can empower women and other underrepresented groups to advocate for equitable pay. Moreover, cross-cultural negotiations demand a nuanced approach, acknowledging diverse communication styles and expectations.

This book also evolves with the changing landscape of work scenarios, such as freelancing and consultancy agreements. It offers insights for professionals managing client budgets and setting competitive contracts. Furthermore, during economic downturns or when weighing multiple offers, strategic negotiation is your ally in securing favorable terms.

The culmination of this book lies in real-world applications and continuous improvement. By studying successful case studies, engaging in mock negotiations, and building a supportive network, you can refine your skills and strategies. This book not only equips you for the negotiation table but also fosters a mindset of growth, empowering you to forge a career path filled with success and fulfillment.

Ultimately, this journey is yours. By transforming the way you think about and conduct negotiations, you lay the foundation for a career filled with opportunities and achievements. The skills developed through this book extend beyond salary discussions and into every aspect of professional interactions, arming you with the tools necessary for lifelong success.

Chapter 1:
The Psychology of Money

Money isn't just a tool for exchanging goods and services; it's a powerful force that shapes decisions, self-worth, and career paths. Whether you're in the midst of salary negotiations or planning your next career leap, understanding the psychological dimensions of money can offer a transformative edge. This chapter unpacks the complex money mindsets that steer our financial choices, from scarcity-driven fears to abundance-oriented aspirations. By recognizing these embedded beliefs, you can confront and overcome financial anxieties that often obstruct confident negotiations. Money is deeply personal—tinged with emotional experiences, cultural backgrounds, and personal narratives. Once you grasp these psychological underpinnings, you can strategically harness them, enhancing your salary negotiation skills with newfound confidence and clarity. Embracing the psychology of money is not just about increasing numbers on a paycheck; it's about paving a path toward financial empowerment and personal fulfillment.

Understanding Money Mindsets

Understanding the nuances of money mindsets can be transformative in salary negotiations. It's not just about dollars and cents; it's about perceptions, beliefs, and attitudes toward money that are deeply ingrained within us. These mindsets shape how we approach negotiations, impacting the strategies we choose and the confidence we project.

A lot of us have narratives about money that we carry from our upbringing or past experiences. Whether we were taught that money is scarce or abundant can profoundly influence our negotiation strategies. Those who grew up hearing phrases like "money doesn't grow on trees" might approach negotiations with a scarcity mindset. This often means fear of asking for what they're worth, believing there's only so much to go around, or concern that the offer on the table might just slip away. On the other hand, an abundance mindset enables one to see opportunities, making it easier to negotiate confidently, believing that there's always more available.

But how do these mindsets translate into negotiable realities? Consider someone who views money as a tool for freedom and security versus someone who sees it as a source of stress and anxiety. The former is likely to enter a negotiation with thoughts of potential growth and leveraging more opportunities. They might focus on collaborating with their employer to reach a mutually beneficial agreement. In contrast, the latter might find the negotiation process daunting, perceiving it as a zero-sum game where any gain on their part might create friction.

To shift your money mindset, reflection is key. Begin by identifying the beliefs that may be holding you back. Ask yourself questions like: How did my parents talk about money? What was my first direct experience with money management? What emotional response do I have when I think about negotiating salary? Recognizing these early influences can be a stepping stone in transforming a limiting mindset into an empowering one.

Once you've identified these beliefs, challenge them. If you catch yourself thinking, "I'm not worth that much," question where that thought comes from. Is it a factual assessment or a lingering echo from a past experience? Re-casting these thoughts in a positive and constructive light can lead to healthier financial habits and attitudes.

Adopting a growth mindset in the context of money means viewing challenges as opportunities to learn rather than insurmountable obstacles. When approaching a salary negotiation, it's valuable to see it not only as a chance to earn more but as an opportunity to develop your articulation and persuasion skills. This mindset doesn't just promise greater financial rewards; it enhances your personal growth, confidence, and negotiation acumen.

Beliefs about self-worth play a pivotal role in negotiations. A positive self-image can empower you to articulate your value confidently within your professional sphere. Conversely, self-doubt can undermine negotiation efforts, leading to settling for less than you deserve. Building self-esteem and recognizing your achievements are therefore crucial steps in fortifying your negotiation mindset. A good practice could be maintaining a success journal where you jot down your accomplishments, big or small, and referring to it before a negotiation.

Another prominent factor intertwining with money mindsets is societal and cultural norms around money. In some cultures, discussing money is seen as taboo, while in others, it's a natural practice from a young age. Understanding not only your cultural stance but also that of your employer or negotiating counterpart can provide insight into how negotiations might unfold. Adapting your approach while respecting these nuances can make for more harmonious and successful outcomes.

The role of financial literacy in shaping money mindsets cannot be ignored. Often, individuals approach salary negotiations with varied levels of understanding regarding market trends, budgeting, and financial implications of different compensation packages. Enhancing your financial literacy equips you with the knowledge needed to understand not just what you're negotiating, but why it's valuable to you, transforming your mindset from a passive recipient to an empowered decision-maker.

Strikingly, one factor affecting money mindsets is emotional wellbeing. Stress, anxiety, and unresolved emotional issues concerning finances can cloud judgment and hinder negotiation capabilities. Practicing mindfulness and stress management techniques can help in maintaining a clear head, allowing for strategic thinking during negotiations. Rather than viewing a negotiation as a battleground, it could be perceived as a meaningful discussion aimed at mutual growth.

In conclusion, understanding and cultivating a healthy money mindset is about more than altering beliefs; it's about adopting a perspective that sees negotiation as an integral part of professional growth. By leveraging past experiences, cultural insights, self-worth, and financial literacy, you can transform your approach to salary negotiations. You'll be better prepared to advocate for yourself and secure the pay that reflects your true value. Recognize the powerful influence of a positive money mindset, and use it as a cornerstone of effective negotiation strategy.

Overcoming Financial Fears

Money is often seen as a source of stress. For many, the mere thought of discussing finances can evoke feelings of anxiety, inadequacy, or even dread. These financial fears are deeply ingrained in our psyche, often rooted in early experiences and societal narratives about wealth and success. However, understanding and overcoming these fears is crucial for navigating salary negotiations successfully.

Financial fears don't just affect negotiations; they're a significant barrier to financial success. Many people carry misconceptions about money, believing that it's not within their control or that discussing money is inherently greedy. Challenging these beliefs is the first step in transforming one's financial mindset. By learning to view money as a tool rather than a stressor, individuals can begin to shift their perceptions and open up new possibilities in their professional lives.

One of the most common fears is the fear of appearing greedy or self-serving. This fear can prevent us from advocating for the salary we deserve. It's important to recognize that asking for fair compensation isn't selfish; it's a reflection of the value we bring to our roles. Reframing this narrative can empower individuals to approach negotiations with confidence, recognizing that every discussion about compensation is an opportunity to affirm self-worth and professional value.

Another pervasive fear is the fear of rejection. The anticipation of hearing "no" can be paralyzing. However, it's essential to remember that rejection isn't a reflection of personal failure. Instead, it's a natural part of the negotiation process. By expecting and preparing for rejections, individuals can remain resilient and focused on long-term goals. Each rejection can become a learning opportunity, offering insights that can be used to refine strategies and approaches for future negotiations.

Financial anxieties often stem from a fear of the unknown. Without a clear understanding of personal finances, market conditions, or negotiation tactics, individuals might feel unprepared and vulnerable. Education plays a pivotal role in dispelling these fears. By arming oneself with knowledge about market rates, industry standards, and negotiation strategies, individuals can approach salary discussions with greater assurance. Knowledge dispels fear, replacing it with the power of informed decision-making.

However, education alone isn't enough. Financial fear often has emotional roots, demanding a more holistic approach. Developing emotional intelligence is critical in recognizing, managing, and responding to one's financial anxieties. Techniques such as mindfulness and cognitive restructuring can help individuals remain calm and focused during negotiations, preventing emotional overreactions and grounding discussions in rational thought and clear communication.

Moreover, seeking mentorship and support can mitigate financial fears. Connecting with experienced professionals or mentors can provide invaluable perspectives and strategies for overcoming specific challenges. Mentors can offer encouragement while sharing insights and experiences that illuminate new paths forward, helping to build the confidence required to face financial negotiations head-on.

Cultivating a positive money mindset is about persistence. It requires acknowledging fears, understanding their origins, and steadily working to replace them with confidence and clarity. With each negotiation, individuals have the opportunity to confront and overcome their financial fears, transforming them into motivational forces driving career growth and success.

The process of overcoming financial fears can feel daunting, but it's achievable. By focusing on preparation, emotional intelligence, and continuous learning, individuals can navigate salary negotiations with greater ease and assurance. Reframing financial fears into opportunities for personal and professional development lays the groundwork for not only effective negotiation but also long-term career satisfaction and growth.

Ultimately, overcoming financial fears is about creating a narrative of empowerment. It's about defining what money means in one's life and aligning financial decisions with personal values and goals. As individuals gain confidence in their ability to manage and negotiate their worth, they become better equipped to achieve their financial aspirations and build fulfilling careers.

Chapter 2:
The Basics of Salary Negotiation

Starting with a strong foundation in salary negotiation is key to ensuring you walk away from the table with what you deserve. It's all about mastering the fundamental skills that underpin successful negotiations, like understanding the value of clarity in communication and the importance of assertiveness without aggression. Picture negotiation as a dance; you're not just demanding, you're collaborating towards a solution that benefits both parties. Everyone has a set of natural negotiation habits, often crafted unconsciously over years in everyday interactions, but when it comes to salary, honing these habits is crucial. Recognizing potential pitfalls, such as hesitancy to state your worth or failure to research, can prevent missteps that cost you financially and professionally. To be effective, engage in introspection first—ask what your salary must fulfill for your satisfaction—and then, outwardly, refine your technique by practicing and learning from each negotiation encounter. This chapter sets the stage, presenting these basics to build your confidence and embolden your approach to discuss pay with assurance.

Essential Negotiation Skills

Salary negotiation isn't just about numbers; it's a delicate dance of persuasion, communication, and strategy. Your ability to navigate this dance hinges on mastering essential negotiation skills. These skills are the foundation of any successful negotiation, whether you're asking for a raise at your current job or negotiating the terms of a new job offer. Let's dive into some of the core skills that can make or break your salary negotiation efforts.

Preparation and Research are at the heart of every successful negotiation. Before you begin any salary discussion, you must know your market value. This means understanding what others in similar roles and industries are earning. Resources like salary surveys and tools can provide that invaluable data. But research is more than just numbers. Look into company performance, industry trends, and even the financial health of the organization you're negotiating with. Such insights can give you a strategic edge and inform your approach.

Active Listening might seem like a soft skill, but it's as powerful as any form of persuasion. In negotiations, listening is just as vital as speaking. It allows you to understand the employer's needs and priorities. Often, by simply listening, you can spot opportunities to align your requests with what the employer values most. This creates openings for compromises that benefit both parties.

Maintaining a clear line of **open communication** is another cornerstone of effective negotiation. This involves articulating your desires and concerns clearly without being confrontational. Transparency fosters trust, making it easier to reach a favorable outcome. More importantly, how you convey your message can significantly impact the negotiation. It's not just what you say, but how you say it.

Once you're communicating openly, the ability to **present your case persuasively** comes into play. This requires storytelling—crafting a narrative where your strengths align with the organization's needs. Be prepared to share specific examples that showcase your contributions and how they translated into tangible outcomes for previous employers. The goal is to make a compelling case that your salary request is not just justified but is the logical choice for both you and the employer.

Emotional intelligence is critical when reading the room. During negotiations, being attuned to verbal and non-verbal cues can provide clues about the other party's thoughts and feelings. This awareness helps in adapting your approach as necessary, ensuring you're not pushing too hard or backing down too quickly. Emotional intelligence allows for more informed reactions and decisions throughout the negotiation process.

It's equally indispensable to be **assertive yet flexible**. Assertiveness ensures you communicate your needs succinctly, ensuring they are heard and taken seriously. But inflexibility can derail negotiations. Being willing to adjust your stance when needed can lead to alternative solutions within the negotiation that still satisfy your goals. The trick is to remain open to various possibilities without compromising your core objectives.

Another vital skill is **problem-solving**. Often, negotiations can boil down to solving a problem that satisfies both parties. Creativity in devising solutions or alternatives is invaluable. Sometimes, a compromise on salary might be acceptable if paired with other benefits, like more vacation days or a flexible work schedule. Be prepared to offer and consider various options.

The skill of **timing** can't be underestimated. Knowing when to present your case or when to hold back is a nuanced art. This entails being aware of organizational cycles such as fiscal years or major company milestones. Timing your negotiations when a company is most receptive to salary discussions can significantly affect the outcome.

Another critical skill is being able to **deal with rejection**. Not every negotiation will end in success, and how you respond to a "no" is telling. Instead of viewing it as the end, see it as an opportunity to open discussions about future possibilities. Remaining professional and composed in the face of rejection reinforces your image as a confident and dedicated individual.

Finally, implementing an **adaptive strategy** means continually assessing the negotiation's progression and being willing to modify your approach based on unfolding dynamics. This skill keeps your negotiation tactics fresh and relevant, allowing you to respond appropriately to changing situations.

To sum up, being well-prepared, an excellent communicator, and emotionally intelligent forms the backbone of essential negotiation skills. Coupled with assertiveness, adaptability, and strategic timing, these capabilities work in unison to bolster your chances of achieving the salary you deserve. Empirical studies and seasoned negotiators note that consistent practice and self-reflection on these skills are instrumental in transforming them into second nature, empowering you to approach any salary negotiation with confidence and poise.

Common Negotiation Pitfalls

Negotiating a salary can be a challenging endeavor, requiring not just preparation but also the finesse to navigate potential pitfalls that often arise. One common mistake is entering negotiations without adequate research or understanding of the industry standard for the role in question. This oversight can lead to undervaluing oneself or missing out on opportunities for a better compensation package. Taking the time to understand the landscape helps in establishing a strong foundation for the discussion.

Another frequent error is focusing too much on the salary figure itself, at the expense of considering the total compensation package. While a high salary sounds appealing, it should be weighed against other benefits such as health insurance, retirement contributions, work-life balance perks, and professional development opportunities.

A holistic view ensures that you're negotiating for a package that's advantageous in the long run.

Overconfidence can also derail negotiations. While confidence is key, it should be balanced with humility and openness. Going into negotiations with an inflated sense of one's worth without considering the employer's perspective or the constraints they might have can result in deadlock. It's vital to remain grounded and engage in a dialogue that's collaborative rather than adversarial.

On the flip side, some individuals suffer from self-doubt and a lack of confidence, which can lead to premature concessions. This often stems from fear of conflict or anxiety about losing the job offer altogether. To counter this, remind yourself that negotiation is a normal and expected part of the hiring process. Preparing well, practicing with friends or mentors, and visualizing success scenarios can bolster your confidence.

Failing to listen actively is another common pitfall. Many individuals focus so intensely on what they plan to say next that they miss key information from the employer. Active listening helps in understanding the employer's needs and priorities, allowing you to tailor your responses in a way that aligns with their goals, which can strengthen your position.

Negotiation styles can also trip up candidates. Some adopt a hardline, aggressive stance, believing it shows strength, but it often alienates potential employers. Conversely, being overly accommodating might come across as lacking in ambition or competence. Finding a balanced approach, where firmness is mixed with flexibility, can lead to better outcomes.

Timing plays a crucial role in negotiations, with errors often occurring in rushing the process or dragging it out for too long. Pushing too quickly can indicate desperation, while being excessively slow might signal indecisiveness. Finding the right timing requires sensitivity to the context of the negotiation and cues from the employer.

One often overlooked pitfall is failing to document agreements and expectations. After reaching a verbal agreement, ensure everything is confirmed in writing. This provides a clear record that can prevent misunderstandings later on and shows professionalism and attention to detail from your side.

Many professionals make the mistake of not preparing adequately for potential "no" responses. Rejection can be hard to handle, but having a plan for such outcomes can turn a potentially demoralizing experience into a learning opportunity. Reflect on the reasons for the rejection, seek constructive feedback, and use the experience to refine future negotiations.

Inadequate emotional control is another hurdle. Negotiations can be tense, but allowing emotions to take over can cloud judgment and lead to hasty decisions. Practicing emotional regulation techniques such as mindfulness, deep breathing, or even taking a moment to pause during the negotiation can help maintain composure and clarity.

Lastly, neglecting to follow up on negotiations can erode the relationship and diminish the impact of a successful agreement. Regardless of the outcome, expressing gratitude and confirming next steps reinforces professionalism and upholds your reputation as a considerate and serious candidate, potentially opening doors for future opportunities.

Avoiding these pitfalls requires a combination of preparation, self-awareness, and adaptability. By recognizing and addressing these challenges heads on, you enhance your ability to negotiate effectively, ensuring you secure the salary and benefits you rightfully deserve.

Chapter 3:
Preparing for Negotiation

As you gear up for your salary negotiations, remember that preparation sets the foundation for success. Start with researching your market value meticulously, which requires dissecting industry trends, regional pay scales, and the specific skill set you bring to the table. Empowered with this knowledge, it's crucial to establish realistic salary goals. These goals should reflect not only your current worth but also your future aspirations, acknowledging the unique contributions you aim to offer. By investing effort into looking up various data points and reflecting on your needs and ambitions, you're cementing your stand with confidence and purpose, ready to approach the negotiation table with a strategic mindset. Your aim is not just to negotiate but to do so with clarity and conviction, ensuring that both the reasoning and the numbers back your requests unmistakably. As you prepare, you'll find this balance of goals and grounded reality acts as your guiding star, propelling you towards favorable outcomes in your negotiation endeavors.

Researching Your Market Value

Understanding your market value is a crucial step in preparing for a salary negotiation. To walk into a negotiation room with confidence, you first need a clear sense of what you're worth in the current market. This knowledge acts as your anchor in negotiations, allowing you to stand firm on your salary expectations. Without it, you're navigating blindly, which can lead to accepting less than you deserve or overestimating your worth and pricing yourself out of opportunities.

So, where do you begin? Start by collecting reliable data on salary ranges for your role within your industry. Utilize resources like online salary calculators, industry reports, and wage statistics. Websites such as Glassdoor, Payscale, and LinkedIn can provide valuable insights. But don't stop there; these resources should just be the start of your research. Remember, online data gives you general figures that might not consider your unique qualifications, experience, or regional economic conditions.

Your professional network is another vital source of information. Reach out to colleagues in similar roles or those who work at your target companies. They can offer firsthand insights that online resources can't. Informal conversations can reveal details about company-specific pay practices or industry salary trends that official reports might miss. Be discrete and respectful when discussing salary information, and offer to share your own insights in return to build mutual trust.

While data is key, context is everything. Consider economic factors that might influence salary ranges in your field. For example, a booming tech industry might elevate software developer salaries, while healthcare might see similar spikes in demand and pay for specialized nurses. On the flip side, economic downturns in a particular sector could depress wages, meaning you'd need to adjust your expectations. The more aware you are of these trends, the smarter your negotiation strategy will be.

Understand the variations across geographic regions. A role in New York City might pay significantly more than the same role in a smaller city due to higher living costs and demand differences. This doesn't mean you should blindly apply national averages to your case.

Reflect on specifics like local job availability, employer demand for your role, and the overall economic health of the region.

Your value isn't just about the market; it's about you—your skills, experience, and accolades. Construct a comprehensive list of your achievements. Reflect on the impact of your work: Did you save your employer money? Did you lead projects that boosted revenues? Did you introduce innovative solutions that revolutionized processes? These elements add depth to your market value and provide concrete examples when discussing why you deserve the pay you're requesting.

Recognize that timing plays a key role. If you've recently received a raise or switched jobs, gathering updated data on your new salary tier and any recent market changes is essential. Conversely, if it's been a long time since your last raise, there might be significant shifts you need to account for, which means recalibrating your understanding of your market worth.

When combining this data, build a salary range rather than a single figure. A range provides flexibility, allowing you to adjust in response to the employer's potential offer while keeping within boundaries you're comfortable with. It also demonstrates openness to negotiation, a trait many employers appreciate.

Be wary of confirmation bias, the tendency to focus on information that validates your preconceived notions. Approach your research with an open mind; you might find your current compensation aligns fairly with market standards, or you may discover room to justify a payday increase. Either way, having objective, comprehensive data empowers you to make informed decisions.

After gathering this data, translate your findings into a narrative that matches your career journey. Practice articulating this amalgam regularly, describing how your skills and experiences align with market expectations. This clarity sharpens your negotiation argument, helps reduce nervousness, and positions you as a savvy professional who knows their value.

Ultimately, researching your market value isn't a one-time event—it's an ongoing process. Regularly update your data and insights as you progress in your career. Stay attuned to industry shifts, advancements in your field, and your growing skill set. This continuous learning not only aids in negotiations but also contributes to a broader understanding of your professional landscape and potential career paths.

Empowered with solid research and articulated self-worth, you enter negotiations with a powerful asset: knowledge. This foundation helps solidify your position, supports your salary requests with evidence, and, ultimately, aids in achieving the compensation package you deserve. Remember, an informed negotiator is a successful negotiator.

Setting Realistic Salary Goals

Setting realistic salary goals is a critical step in preparing for any negotiation. It lays the foundation for your approach and helps align your expectations with market realities. Establishing a target that's both ambitious and attainable requires a strategic blend of introspection, research, and pragmatism. Knowing your worth is essential, but anchoring it in reality ensures you negotiate confidently without overshooting or selling yourself short.

Understanding your market value is not just about analyzing salary data; it's about aligning your skills, experience, and potential with industry standards. You can't simply pick a number out of thin air, nor should you rely only on anecdotal advice. Begin by tapping into reliable resources like salary surveys, industry reports, and professional networks. Websites like Glassdoor and Payscale offer valuable insights, but they should be just one part of your research toolkit. Cross-reference these figures with insights from industry contacts and mentors to form a well-rounded view of your market value.

But numbers alone don't capture your full value. Consider the unique attributes and experiences you bring to the table. Do you possess niche skills that are in high demand? Have you achieved specific results in past roles? These are your leverage points. While research gives you a baseline, personal achievements and unique skills could push you beyond the average market rates. So, weigh what sets you apart as heavily as what the market dictates.

Once you've gathered data, it's time to critically assess your current position. Reflect on your career trajectory: How have your roles evolved over time? Are there gaps in your expertise that need addressing? Awareness of your strengths, weaknesses, and the areas you need to improve can guide your salary goals and help you present a compelling case. Construct a narrative that not only highlights your past successes but also positions you as an asset for future growth.

When setting your salary goals, aim for a range rather than a fixed number. This flexibility allows room for negotiation and demonstrates a willingness to collaborate. The lower end of your range should be the minimum you're willing to accept, while the upper end should represent the ideal salary you believe your skills and market research justify. This approach not only protects your interests but also empowers the employer with options, fostering a more constructive dialogue.

It's crucial to remain adaptable to changing situations. Economic fluctuations or shifts within your industry could impact salary trends, requiring you to revisit and adjust your expectations. Stay updated on these dynamics, and be prepared to recalibrate your goals in response. Demonstrating an understanding of economic and industry conditions can also strengthen your position during negotiations, showing that your expectations are well-informed and reasonable.

Equally important is considering non-monetary compensation. Benefits like flexible work hours, remote work options, professional development opportunities, and comprehensive healthcare plans can significantly bolster your overall compensation package. When salary goals seem unreachable, these perks can bridge the gap, ensuring you still receive the value you deserve.

A critical step in setting realistic salary goals is acknowledging any biases that might influence your perceptions. Self-doubt or imposter syndrome can often lead to undervaluing oneself. If you find these thoughts creeping in, revisit your accomplishments, seek feedback from trusted colleagues, or even consider professional coaching to boost your self-assessment skills. Identifying and correcting these biases will ensure that your salary goals truly reflect your worth.

As you hone your salary targets, practice articulating them clearly and confidently. It's one thing to set a goal; it's another to convincingly communicate it in a negotiation setting. Engage in mock negotiations with peers or mentors to refine your pitch, incorporating clear evidence from your research and personal achievements. This practice not only solidifies your goals but also prepares you to advocate for them persuasively.

Remember, setting realistic salary goals is about striking a balance between aspiration and realism. It requires a harmonious blend of data and introspection, supported by a solid understanding of your unique value proposition. With well-defined goals, you're not just heading into negotiations prepared—you're entering with the confidence needed to advocate effectively for the salary you deserve.

Chapter 4:
Building Confidence

Building confidence is the cornerstone of effective salary negotiation. It's about transforming the nervous energy that comes with money discussions into a powerful, persuasive presence. Confidence doesn't just happen overnight; it requires a thoughtful blend of preparation, self-awareness, and practice. Start by understanding your worth and the value you bring to the table, which forms the foundation upon which you can confidently stand. Engage in role-playing scenarios to simulate negotiation environments and refine your communication skills, which can in turn reduce anxiety and build self-assuredness. Techniques such as positive visualization and affirmations can also play a crucial role in fostering a mindset geared towards success. By fortifying your confidence, you're more likely to advocate effectively for yourself, turning potential apprehension into an unshakeable belief in your own potential, paving the way for achieving the compensation you deserve.

Confidence-Boosting Techniques

Negotiating your salary often feels like stepping onto a high-stakes stage. Whether you're asking for a raise or discussing the terms for a new job, confidence is your foundation. Without it, even the most compelling arguments can crumble. Confidence isn't just a personality trait; it's a skill you can build and refine, and it plays a pivotal role in how others perceive your worth.

Acknowledging your achievements is the first step in boosting your confidence. Make it a habit to record accomplishments, feedback from peers, and significant projects you've completed. This personal inventory serves as tangible evidence of your contributions and value. Reflect on these whenever self-doubt creeps in, transforming them into a reminder of your capabilities and successes.

Visualization is another powerful technique. Before going into a negotiation, visualize yourself succeeding. Imagine the scenario, the questions they'll ask, and your poised responses. See yourself as calm and confident. This mental rehearsal primes your brain for how you want to perform and reduces anxiety. Athletes and performers use similar techniques to enhance their performance, and you can do the same.

Practice makes perfect is a phrase many of us know, but deliberate practice is what makes the difference. Engage in mock negotiation sessions with a trusted friend or mentor. This isn't just about rehearsing lines; it's about getting comfortable with the back-and-forth dialogue and learning to think on your feet. The more familiar you become with negotiation settings, the less intimidating they feel, gradually boosting your confidence.

Another key technique is setting clear goals. Know precisely what you want to achieve in the negotiation and outline specific objectives. When your goals are clear, you project certainty and command greater respect. This clarity not only boosts your confidence but also ensures that you advocate effectively for yourself.

The power of positive affirmations should not be underestimated. Daily, remind yourself of your worth and capabilities. This simple habit can shift your mindset from uncertainty to assurance. Instead of focusing on potential failures, affirm your potential and readiness to succeed. Statements like "I am capable of negotiating the salary I deserve" can reshape your self-perception over time.

Furthermore, developing a growth mindset can significantly impact your confidence levels. Embrace the idea that skills, including negotiation prowess, can be cultivated through effort and perseverance. When you view challenges as opportunities for growth rather than threats, confidence flows naturally as you navigate negotiations with a learning-oriented perspective.

Your posture and speech can also alter how confident you feel. Non-verbal cues have a direct influence on your mindset and the impressions you create. Stand tall, maintain eye contact, and project your voice with clarity. These physical cues not only affect how others perceive you but also reinforce your own sense of confidence. Even subtle changes in posture can have profound effects on how you think and feel about your capabilities.

Building a strong support network is crucial for sustaining confidence. Surround yourself with colleagues, mentors, and friends who encourage and bolster your self-esteem. This network can provide constructive feedback, offer encouragement, and remind you of your value when you're feeling uncertain. Knowing that others believe in you can be a significant confidence booster when gearing up for tough negotiations.

Finally, embracing self-compassion in moments of self-doubt can help preserve your confidence. Recognize that everyone experiences setbacks and challenges. It's not about avoiding failure but learning from it. Allow yourself to be imperfect without letting it undermine your self-worth. This kind of resilience is a cornerstone of lasting confidence.

By integrating these confidence-boosting techniques into your routine, you can create a powerful foundation for any negotiation. Confidence doesn't just happen overnight—it's built through intentional practice and mindset adjustments. As you hone these techniques, you'll find that entering negotiations with confidence becomes second nature, empowering you to secure the salary you deserve.

Role-Playing Scenarios

Role-playing scenarios are an invaluable tool when it comes to building confidence in salary negotiations. By simulating real-life dialogue, these exercises allow you to practice and refine your negotiation tactics in a risk-free environment. Think of it as a dress rehearsal before the main performance, providing an opportunity to iron out flaws and enhance your strengths. In the high-stakes world of salary talks, preparation is indeed half the battle.

One of the key advantages of role-playing is that it allows you to experience both sides of the negotiation table. By switching roles between negotiator and employer, you gain insights into the thought processes and tactics that might be used against you, helping you anticipate and craft effective counter-strategies. This dual perspective is not just an exercise in empathy; it's a strategic advantage that can tip the scales in your favor.

To start, recruit a role-play partner. This could be a trusted colleague, friend, or mentor who is willing to engage in this exercise with you. The ideal partner is someone who can challenge you by presenting diverse scenarios and responses. These role-plays should mimic realistic interactions as closely as possible, using actual figures and circumstances you might encounter. Remember to focus on the authenticity of the scenario to ensure the practice is meaningful.

Set up your scenarios by clearly defining the roles, context, and objectives. For instance, one scenario might involve you as a mid-level manager negotiating a raise in a growing tech company. The role-player acting as your "boss" could present possible firm stances like budget constraints or performance metrics. In another scenario, you might take on the role of a new hire negotiating an offer, considering factors such as market salary rates and benefits.

Engaging in role-playing isn't solely about practicing what you'll say; it's also about learning to read the room. Pay attention to non-verbal cues such as tone, posture, and gestures. These often reveal more than words themselves and can provide critical clues about how your arguments are being received. By attuning to these subtle signals, you can adapt your strategy dynamically during the actual negotiation.

As you role-play, emphasize scenario diversity. Simulate different negotiation styles, from cooperative approaches to more competitive ones. For example, practice handling both an agreeable employer who responds positively to your requests and one who is resistant or even dismissive. This variety equips you to navigate real-world conversations deftly, no matter who is on the other side of the table.

Another key aspect of role-playing is feedback. After each session, discuss what worked and what didn't. Constructive feedback should be specific, focusing on areas for improvement and strategies for overcoming challenges. Was your tone confident and assertive or did it come off as aggressive? Did you effectively communicate your value or falter under pressure? This process of reflection and adjustment is essential for continuous improvement.

Incorporate psychological principles you've learned into these role-plays. Utilize techniques like the anchoring effect, where you set a strong initial position, or apply principles from cognitive framing to present your salary requests in the most compelling light. The goal is to ingrain these tactics into your muscle memory so that you can employ them naturally during an actual negotiation.

Remember, this exercise is not about memorizing lines but developing a flexible skill set that you can draw upon instinctively. Genuine confidence stems not from knowing exactly what to say but from knowing how to respond when taken off guard. By the end of a thorough role-playing regimen, you should feel more equipped to handle unexpected turns with composure and agility.

Consider recording your sessions. Reviewing your performance can provide unexpected insights into both strengths and areas needing improvement. This can be particularly effective if you notice recurring patterns in your responses. Often, we are unaware of our habitual tendencies until we see them objectively.

Role-playing scenarios aren't just for pre-negotiation preparation. They're a sustainable practice that can continue to refine your skills over time. Subsequent role-plays can revisit past scenarios with the benefit of hindsight, allowing for further development of techniques and greater familiarity with different negotiation dynamics.

Ultimately, the aim of role-playing is to make the action of negotiating feel less daunting. Repetition breeds familiarity, and familiarity breeds confidence. When faced with the real thing, having effectively rehearsed numerous scenarios can ease nerves and help you deliver your case convincingly.

Even seasoned negotiators benefit from periodic role-playing to maintain their edge. Skills can grow rusty without practice, and the landscape of negotiation is ever-evolving. New strategies emerge, and so too do new styles of counter-negotiation from employers. A regular regimen of role-play keeps you sharp, adaptable, and ready for any challenge.

In conclusion, role-playing scenarios are a powerful way to build confidence for salary negotiations. They foster a deep understanding of negotiation dynamics through practice and reflection. By dedicating time to these simulations, you cultivate the confidence and skill to enter any salary discussion with poise and determination, ultimately achieving the compensation you deserve.

Chapter 5:
Communicating Effectively

Communication is at the heart of every successful salary negotiation. It's not just about choosing the right words; it's about delivering them with clarity, conviction, and a deep understanding of the dynamics at play. When negotiating salary, it's crucial to master verbal cues, which convey confidence and assertiveness without aggression. Equally important is the power of active listening, which goes beyond simply hearing words to truly understanding the employer's perspective, concerns, and priorities. By skillfully balancing articulate expression with attentive listening, you create an open channel for dialogue, reduce misunderstandings, and build rapport. These communication strategies not only facilitate more effective negotiations but also empower you to articulate your value persuasively, making your case with nuance and strength. With practice, you'll find that these techniques become second nature, equipping you to navigate negotiations with a calm, strategic confidence that leaves a lasting impression.

Mastering Verbal Cues

In salary negotiations, words possess immense power, and the manner in which they are delivered can significantly impact the outcome. Understanding verbal cues is vital, as these are not just about what you say but how you say it. The nuances of tone, pitch, and pace paint a more comprehensive picture than words alone. In this essential chapter, we're diving into the art of mastering verbal cues to enhance your salary negotiation skills.

Verbal cues are your arsenal in negotiations. They are not just about pronouncing words correctly or speaking fluently. The real magic lies in how your words resonate with others and foster connection. Let's start by considering the basic elements: tone, speed, and volume. Each plays a distinct role in how your message is conveyed and perceived. Speaking in a calm and measured tone can convey confidence and assertiveness, a crucial advantage when discussing compensation. On the other hand, an excessively high volume or rapid speech may unintentionally communicate anxiety or desperation.

To ensure your verbal communication aligns with your negotiation goals, practice active modulation of your tone to express not only your intentions but also your confidence in stating your worth. Think of the storyteller who captures an audience by varying voice pitch and rhythm to maintain engagement. Similarly, nuanced verbal delivery can sway a salary discussion in your favor, making your narrative compelling and persuasive.

Listening actively to the verbal cues of others is equally important. Silence is as valuable as speech and can be strategic in driving a conversation. Pausing thoughtfully rather than replying immediately provides space for reflection and careful response formulation. During negotiations, a well-placed pause may prompt the other party to fill the silence, often with beneficial information or concessions. This tactic can be instrumental in revealing an employer's unspoken thoughts or reservations about your salary proposal.

The art of mirroring is another technique skilled negotiators use to build rapport and demonstrate empathy. By subtly adopting the verbal styles of the person you're negotiating with, you create a sense of alignment and understanding. This doesn't mean mimicking their speech exactly but echoing their language patterns or phrases to create familiarity. The psychology behind mirroring suggests it encourages the other party to be more receptive to your stance and increases the likelihood of a favorable negotiation outcome.

Moreover, adapting your verbal style to the context of the conversation can further enhance the impact of what you're trying to convey. For example, if the negotiation turns tense, you can deliberately soften your tone and slow your speech to introduce calm. Conversely, increasing energy and enthusiasm when discussing mutual benefits can inject positivity, keeping the dialogue constructive and forward-focused. A shift in verbal dynamics can transform a stagnant negotiation, inviting solutions rather than impasse.

Your choice of words themselves—apart from their auditory qualities—also bears influence. Using action-oriented and assertive language is crucial in reinforcing your position. For instance, phrases like "I am confident that..." or "I propose..." exhibit decisiveness and authority. Clear, concise language eliminates ambiguity, avoiding potential misinterpretations that could derail a negotiation. At the same time, it is essential to balance assertiveness with politeness. Employing courteous language fosters respect and ensures that negotiations remain professional.

Incorporating questions into your dialogue can effectively uncover needs and priorities while maintaining control of the conversation. Open-ended questions initiate dialogue and offer insight into the employer's perspective, allowing you to adjust your strategy accordingly. For example, asking, "Could you tell me more about the budget considerations for this role?" not only showcases your understanding but also positions you as proactive and engaged. Negotiation is not solely about putting forward demands; it's about cultivating a dialogue for mutual benefit.

Mastering verbal cues requires continuous practice and awareness, much like honing a musical instrument. Record yourself during practice negotiations to evaluate your tone and timing. Pay attention to feedback from peers or mentors who can offer insights into your verbal delivery. Acknowledge that each conversation is an opportunity to refine your skills—each exchange brings you closer to articulating the value you bring with confidence and precision.

The mastery of verbal cues doesn't guarantee an immediate victory in every negotiation, but it equips you with the capability to steer conversations constructively toward your desired outcome. By focusing on verbal skills as part of your negotiation toolkit, you're better positioned to navigate the complexities of salary discussions. The effectiveness of your spoken words can be the difference between settling for an offer and achieving the pay that truly reflects your worth and potential.

The journey of mastering verbal cues intertwines deeply with the other facets of negotiation outlined in this book. It enhances your ability to listen actively, frame your case compellingly, and even understand the emotional undercurrents present in the room. It sets the foundation for a more profound comprehension of the negotiation landscape, amplifying your ability to not just seek but secure the most favorable salary terms.

The Power of Active Listening

Active listening is the unsung hero of effective communication, particularly in the delicate dance of salary negotiations. Often overlooked in favor of more overt negotiation tactics, the ability to truly listen can be a distinguishing factor between settling for a standard offer and securing a compensation package that reflects your true worth. But what does it mean to actively listen, and how does it translate into more effective negotiations?

At its core, active listening involves fully concentrating, understanding, and responding to a speaker—going beyond simply hearing words to grasp the meaning behind them. This approach cultivates trust, builds rapport, and positions you as a cooperative counterpart rather than an adversary. When negotiating your salary, demonstrating that you're engaged and interested in what your employer has to say can significantly shift the dynamic in your favor.

The first step in practicing active listening is to focus entirely on the speaker. This means setting aside your own agenda temporarily and tuning into their words and body language. An active listener gives verbal and non-verbal cues like nodding, maintaining eye contact, and providing affirmations such as "I see," or "That's interesting," to show engagement. When discussions become heated or tense—and they often do in negotiations—grounding yourself in these fundamental techniques can help maintain an open line of communication.

It's crucial to understand the power of silence in a negotiation setting. Giving space for the other party to express their thoughts without interruption not only shows respect but often leads them to reveal more information than they initially intended. Silence can be particularly powerful when discussing salary adjustments—it might encourage the employer to disclose budget limitations or offer alternative benefits, such as flexible hours or bonuses, that hadn't been put on the table yet.

Listening actively also involves asking clarifying questions. These are inquiries that help ensure both parties are on the same wavelength and that there are no misunderstandings. For example, if an employer hesitates about a salary range, you might ask, "Could you elaborate on how you arrived at these figures?" Such questions help uncover revealing details about a company's pay structure and priorities.

Beyond asking questions, paraphrasing or summarizing what has been said can reinforce understanding. For instance, reflecting back a statement like, "So, what I'm hearing is that there are budget constraints this quarter, but performance-related bonuses are a possibility next year," demonstrates that you're not only listening but comprehending the nuances behind the words. This practice can foster a collaborative atmosphere where both parties feel their viewpoints are acknowledged.

Another benefit of active listening is its ability to defuse tension. When negotiations hit a stalemate, listening can serve as a bridge over troubled waters. By acknowledging an employer's concerns without immediately trying to counteract them, you subtly guide the conversation away from confrontation and towards resolution. Empathy, a key component of active listening, allows you to respond not just with words but with an understanding of the emotions behind the other party's position.

Active listening is equally important when reading between the lines. Employers often communicate important messages indirectly. A hesitant tone or an intentional redirection can signal more than what's being explicitly stated. Picking up on such subtleties can give you an edge in adjusting your negotiation tactics in real time, making your case stronger and more adaptable.

It's essential to consider that active listening aligns well with our psychological need for social validation and understanding. When you listen to an employer with intent and respect, you're subtly encouraging them to reciprocate. This balanced exchange not only facilitates a better negotiation outcome but also enhances your professional reputation as a thoughtful, collaborative individual long after the talks have concluded.

Incorporating active listening into your negotiation skill set does not happen overnight, but the effort is well worth it. Start by practicing in daily interactions before applying these skills in a negotiation context. The ability to listen effectively is just as crucial as crafting the perfect offer or understanding market value, if not more so. It elevates you from a mere participant in the negotiation to an active architect, strategically guiding the conversation to favorable shores.

To master the art of active listening, be patient and curious. Realize that every conversation is an opportunity to practice this skill and improve. As you hone your ability to listen actively, you'll find negotiations becoming less daunting and more rewarding. You'll walk away with not just an agreement but a deeper connection and understanding that could pave the way for future opportunities. Remember, the most successful negotiators are not those who talk the most but those who use the power of active listening to talk—and act—most effectively.

As you prepare for your next negotiation, make a conscious effort to listen actively. It can transform interactions and lead to outcomes that satisfy both your professional ambitions and personal growth. The power of active listening is immense, and when wielded effectively, it can indeed become your ultimate negotiation tool.

Chapter 6:
Timing and Strategy

Having the right strategy during salary negotiations is critical, but equally important is knowing *when* to make your move. Timing can be the difference between success and missed opportunity. Strategic planning begins with identifying optimal moments to open salary discussions, whether during annual reviews or when you've recently delivered exceptional performance. It's essential to align your timing with the company's financial cycle. Strategic planning involves gathering insights into organizational cues that indicate readiness, such as budget reviews or new financial cycles. Couple this with preparation, and you can tailor your approach to maximize impact. Crafting a strategy with these components empowers you with control and leverage, enhancing the chances for a successful negotiation. Remember, a well-timed negotiation with a solid strategy at its core is not just about securing a better salary, but about deepening your understanding of the negotiation process itself.

Knowing When to Negotiate

Timing is everything, they say, and when it comes to salary negotiations, this adage holds immense truth. Negotiating at the right moment can be the difference between securing the salary you aspire to and settling for less than you deserve. So, how does one recognize the opportune moment to initiate these crucial discussions? It involves a combination of understanding the dynamics within your company and being attuned to personal readiness, as well as external market conditions.

First, let's delve into the company's financial cycle and staffing needs. Many organizations have specific times of the year when they review budgets, grant salary increases, or discuss bonuses. Aligning your negotiation with these cycles can work to your advantage. For instance, approaching the topic shortly after you've wrapped up a highly successful project can bolster your case. Timing your conversation around these moments can show that you're in sync with company priorities, potentially making them more receptive to your request.

Equally important is your personal timing. Are you adding significant value to your team or company that warrants a discussion about your compensation? Reflect on your recent achievements, additional responsibilities you've taken on, or professional milestones reached. If you're consistently exceeding expectations, it's likely time to talk numbers. However, self-awareness is key; jumping into negotiations without enough recent accomplishments to back your case could weaken your position.

External market conditions can also dictate when to negotiate. If your industry is experiencing growth or there is a high demand for professionals with your skills, it's a prime opportunity to request a pay raise. Research job market trends and salary benchmarks for your position to ensure you're well-informed. On the flip side, during times of economic downturn, demonstrating an understanding of market challenges while stating your case thoughtfully may be crucial in setting realistic expectations.

Now, shift perspective and consider the implications of poor timing. Engaging in negotiation discussions during a company's restructuring, layoffs, or financial cutbacks could be perceived as tone-deaf. Awareness of your organization's current state and showing respect for its circumstances can ensure you manage the timing of your negotiation wisely.

Moreover, timing isn't just about sensing the right moment in the calendar year or economic cycle; it's also about emotional timing. Approaching your manager after they've faced a challenging day or during a particularly stressful period might not yield the best results. Gauge their mood and stress levels by cultivating active listening skills and developing emotional intelligence – topics we will explore further in later chapters.

Sometimes, the simplest yet most overlooked aspect of timing is being patient for the opportune moment. The eagerness to negotiate might lead you to rush into conversations prematurely. Practice patience, allowing the timing to naturally evolve rather than forcing it. This patience will also reflect your composure, another persuasive quality in negotiation scenarios.

Astute negotiators also recognize that successful timing involves planning secondary strategies to leverage opportunities as they arise. For instance, sharing your salary expectations shortly after receiving a job offer can be conducive if you can weave your request into the overall conversation about your role and responsibilities. Being strategic and ready to capitalize on these windows of opportunity lays the groundwork for successful timing.

When examining timing, don't overlook internal readiness and confidence level. Even with perfect external conditions, if you're not mentally prepared to negotiate, your discussions may falter. Hence, building confidence in negotiations is indispensable; role-play scenarios, visualizing success, and self-affirmation can all fortify your internal readiness. Remember, confidence is contagious, and projecting assurance can sway discussions in your favor.

Remember that good timing is not merely about synchronizing with the external environment; it's also an inner game. Balancing personal aspirations with professional acumen and ensuring the timing is right from every angle can empower you to achieve your salary negotiation goals effectively. When preparation meets the perfect moment, successful negotiations ensue, turning aspirations into reality.

Knowing when to negotiate is an art form. It requires an amalgamation of observation, reflection, market awareness, emotional intelligence, and strategic patience. As you continue through this journey to boost your salary negotiation skills, take time to master the craft of recognizing and seizing the moment, making informed decisions that lead to the pay you rightfully deserve.

Strategic Planning for Salary Talks

Timing is crucial when approaching salary negotiation; it's not just about when to negotiate but also how to structure your strategy around it. The essence of strategic planning for salary talks lies in aligning your negotiation goals with opportune moments and crafting a comprehensive approach that considers your long-term career trajectory.

Your initial step in strategic planning should involve creating a blueprint of your career aspirations and aligning these with your salary objectives. It's essential to be clear about not only your immediate financial needs but also your long-term professional growth. This understanding enables you to approach negotiations not just as a means to an end but as a critical step in a larger career strategy.

Identifying the right moment to hold salary talks is an art form. Timing your negotiation could make a significant difference in the outcome. Consider embarking on these discussions following successful project completions or notable achievements that highlight your value to the organization. It's at these points that your contributions are most fresh in the minds of decision-makers, allowing you to leverage recent successes in your negotiation talks.

Preparation is pivotal. Conducting thorough research on industry standards and competitors' packages is a must. This information provides you with a solid foundation to gauge how your request sits within the market context, positioning you as knowledgeable and prepared. Utilizing tools and technology, as discussed in later chapters, to gather detailed insights can elevate your planning process.

Understanding the company's fiscal calendar can also play a significant role in your planning. Organizations often allocate budget increases at specific times, such as at the end of a fiscal year or after quarterly reviews. By positioning your negotiation at these junctures, you align your request with the company's financial planning processes, increasing the likelihood of a favorable response.

Approach your salary talk with a strategy that includes a mix of assertiveness and flexibility. Craft a clear, coherent pitch that articulates your achievements, market research, and career aspirations. Yet, be prepared to listen actively and respond to the employer's perspective. This balance of assertiveness and openness helps build a collaborative, rather than confrontational, dialogue.

Expressing your value proposition clearly and persuasively is fundamental. It's about demonstrating how your skills and contributions align with the organization's goals, making your raise not just a personal gain but a mutual benefit. More on crafting this pitch is covered in later chapters, focusing on thorough preparation and clear articulation of your case.

Incorporate flexibility into your strategy. Being open to negotiating other aspects of your compensation if salary adjustments aren't immediately possible can be an effective strategy. This could include performance-based bonuses, additional benefits, or opportunities for professional development that align with your career goals.

Practicing your negotiation technique through role-playing scenarios can help boost your confidence and improve your delivery. Anticipating potential employer objections and preparing your responses ensures that you're not caught off-guard, allowing you to maintain control of the conversation.

Finally, consider the broader implications of your negotiation strategy within your career. Each successful negotiation builds your reputation, not only as an effective negotiator but as a professional who understands their worth and aligns it with strategic company goals. Through careful planning and execution, you not only enhance your immediate position but also set the stage for future growth.

By employing these strategies, you'll walk into salary discussions armed with the confidence and insight necessary to achieve your desired outcome. Planning strategically turns the negotiation from a daunting task into a calculated step forward in your career, blending timing with tactical preparation.

Chapter 7:
Navigating Employer Tactics

As you journey through the landscape of salary negotiations, understanding employer tactics becomes a crucial skill that can set you apart. Employers often have a set of strategies aimed at maintaining control and securing the best deal for the company, such as downplaying budget constraints or subtly deploying the infamous lowball offer. Recognizing these techniques requires a sharp eye and a strategic mindset. Instead of falling into their traps, use their tactics as signals to navigate the conversation creatively. For instance, when faced with a lowball offer, counter with well-researched data and a compelling narrative of your contributions and potential value. Employing this approach not only shifts the conversation back to your strengths but can also transform the negotiation from a standoff into a collaborative discussion. Remember, the goal isn't just securing a better salary—it's also about demonstrating your worth and establishing a respectful, advantageous relationship with your employer.

Recognizing Employer Negotiation Techniques

In the intricate dance of salary negotiations, understanding employer tactics is pivotal. Employers, like seasoned negotiators, often deploy an array of strategies to maintain control and secure favorable outcomes for themselves. However, recognizing these techniques can empower you to respond effectively and tilt the scales in your favor. As you proceed, it's crucial to balance assertiveness with diplomacy, ensuring that both parties feel heard and respected.

One prevalent strategy is the **"Good Cop, Bad Cop"** approach. It's a time-tested tactic where one party adopts a stern demeanor while another adopts a more accommodating stance. This can psychologically manipulate candidates into seeing the accommodating party as an ally, nudging them into agreeing to the terms presented. Recognizing this strategy allows you to remain steady. Acknowledge both perspectives, verify any claims with facts, and negotiate on specific terms without getting swayed by personalities.

Employers might also employ **anchoring**, a principle borrowed from behavioral economics. By introducing an initial low or high number, they set the negotiation baseline. This initial anchor can significantly impact the ultimate outcome. Savvy negotiators counteract this by presenting their anchor first, drawing from well-researched market data to justify it. If an anchor is already set, challenge it with data and explain why your expectations differ.

A more subtle technique is the **"Take it or Leave it"** tactic, an ultimatum designed to corner you into making a quick decision. By insisting that there's no room for negotiation, employers attempt to pressure candidates into compliance. Knowing this, you can defuse its impact by expressing appreciation for the offer while indicating your need for more time to consider. Often, a polite insistence on needing time recalibrates the negotiation, opening new avenues for dialogue.

Another common strategy is to **speak vaguely about the full compensation package**. By shifting focus from the base salary to non-salary benefits, employers might attempt to obscure less favorable terms with attractive fringe benefits. While benefits are indeed vital, it's crucial to quantify these perks in monetary terms and compare them against the market standard. Ensure your judgment of the offer considers both salary and benefits independently to get a clear picture of what's truly on the table.

The stratagem of **"silent treatment"** is a classic. It functions on the discomfort silence often creates. After articulating demands or expectations, candidates might find prolonged silence unnerving, prompting them to amend their propositions or concede too quickly. Embrace the silence instead. Allow it to serve as a pause for both parties to process information. Use the time to reassess your position and prepare for the subsequent course of the negotiation.

Employers may also opt for **"the appeal to budget constraints"**. During discussions, financial limitations might be highlighted as the reason behind a tight offer, invoking a sense of realism or guilt in candidates. To navigate this effectively, shift the focus away from constraints and toward your value and potential contributions. Propose alternative structures, such as performance-based increments or promotions tied to project successes, which allow gratification for both ends without breaching budgetary boundaries.

A more direct tactic is the **"limited-time offer"**, where a deadline is imposed to pressurize quick agreement. While a time constraint might be genuine, it's often used to create a false sense of urgency. Maintain your composure by analyzing if the time limitation is legitimate. If needed, request more time politely, explaining your need for thorough consideration. In most cases, an extension is granted if the employer is genuinely interested.

Lastly, the approach of **"downplaying other opportunities"** emerges when an employer seeks to diminish the allure of competitive offers. They may underline the risks of shifting companies frequently or question other companies' stability. It's crucial to stay grounded in your research. Reflect on the pros and cons of all opportunities, acknowledging market perceptions but making a decision aligned with your career goals and values.

Equally important is how you approach negotiations. Maintain an open, communicative stance, avoiding giving away too much at once. Allow yourself moments to pause the discussion, perhaps to consult with a mentor or to realign your standpoint privately. Doing so prevents impulsive decisions and enhances your confidence.

Empowered with knowledge of these strategies, you are better prepared to navigate the nuanced terrain of employer negotiations. These insights enable you to maintain clarity and assertiveness, paving the way for a mutually beneficial agreement where your value is recognized and adequately compensated. Remember, negotiations are not merely a test of wills but a journey towards a shared understanding and mutual gain.

Countering Lowball Offers

Encountering a lowball offer during a salary negotiation can feel like hitting a brick wall. It's unexpected, and if you're not prepared, it can easily derail the conversation. However, this tactic is not uncommon, and employers may use it for various reasons—testing your negotiation skills, gauging your market knowledge, or simply to control budget constraints. Recognizing and countering these offers requires both a strategic mindset and an understanding of negotiation dynamics.

First, it's crucial to maintain composure. Low initial offers can trigger an emotional response, leaving you feeling undervalued or insulted. However, reacting emotionally can cloud your judgment and weaken your position. Instead, view the offer as a part of the negotiation dance. It's not the end, but merely a beginning. Like any negotiation, it's influenced by several psychological principles, where your response can strategically reset expectations.

Begin by evaluating the offer objectively. Take time to consider what might have led the employer to propose this particular starting point. Are they constrained by budget limitations, or is it a test of your negotiation abilities? Dive into some introspection, and don't hesitate to ask for details. A simple request for the employer to explain how they arrived at the offer can provide valuable insights into their priorities and flexibility.

Next, it's essential to base your counterargument on well-researched facts. Data becomes your ally in these conversations. Having a clear understanding of your worth and market standards fortifies your position. Gather salary data for similar roles in the industry and region to back your counteroffer. Highlighting specific achievements and how they align with the company's objectives can also make a compelling case for why their initial offer undershoots your value.

A useful tactic is to reframe the conversation. Instead of viewing it as a confrontation, transform it into a collaborative problem-solving session. Express your enthusiasm for the role and reiterate your commitment to contributing to the company's success. Then, subtly shift the focus to aligning your compensation with industry standards and your capability to deliver exceptional results. This not only softens the negotiation atmosphere but also positions you as a partner rather than an adversary.

Communicate your counteroffer with clarity and conviction. Articulate your reasoning logically, ensuring the employer understands that your ask is neither arbitrary nor unrealistic. Acknowledge their constraints respectfully, suggesting alternative solutions that could work within their framework, such as performance bonuses or reevaluation periods. This approach shows flexibility and a keen sense of empathy, qualities that can strengthen your professional rapport.

Moreover, it's imperative to be patient and strategic about timing. An immediate counter can appear reactive, whereas a thoughtful one demonstrates deliberate consideration. Allowing some time before you respond also gives the employer room to ponder their initial proposal and anticipate your counteroffer. Rushing to close the deal might leave money on the table, so take a moment to strategize your next move.

While using logic and data is vital, don't underestimate the power of storytelling. Humanize the negotiation by sharing your professional journey, connecting your experiences directly to the value you bring. Draw tangible lines between your skills and their company's needs, making it hard for them to overlook what you contribute.

Understanding the employer's perspective is another critical aspect. Employers might use lowball offers as a filtering tool to identify those who accept without contest or those willing to engage in negotiation. Showing you're the latter projects tremendous confidence and showcases your negotiation acumen, a valued skill in any employee.

Finally, don't shy away from exploring additional benefits outside the salary structure. This could be an opportunity to negotiate for better work-life balance options, additional vacation days, or professional development opportunities. These perks often hold significant value and reflect the organization's willingness to invest in their employees beyond monetary terms.

In summary, countering lowball offers involves a blend of emotional intelligence and hard facts. Market research, effective communication, patience, and an understanding of psychological principles form the arsenal you'll deploy. Approach each negotiation as a learning experience and an opportunity to refine your skills, keeping in mind that every interaction adds to your cumulative expertise in securing the compensation you deserve.

Chapter 8:
Leveraging Psychological Principles

When it comes to salary negotiations, tapping into psychological principles can significantly tilt the scales in your favor. It's not just about numbers and facts; understanding human behavior adds a valuable dimension to your strategy. Concepts like the anchoring effect, where the first offer often sets the stage for all subsequent discussions, can be powerful if used wisely. Similarly, reciprocity, the idea that people tend to return favors, can be leveraged to build rapport and goodwill with your employer. By recognizing these behaviors, you can navigate negotiations with a keen awareness, allowing you to influence outcomes subtly yet effectively. Embrace these insights not merely as tactics but as tools that, when wielded skillfully, can empower you to negotiate the salary you deserve and accelerate your career progression.

The Anchoring Effect in Negotiations

Often in negotiations, the first number mentioned holds a powerful influence over the subsequent discussion. This phenomenon, known as the "anchoring effect," can significantly impact salary negotiations. Understanding how to use anchoring to your advantage can give you an edge when aiming to secure a salary rise. What's remarkable about anchoring is its subtlety. It's not just about choosing the right opening figure—it's about understanding the psychological dynamics at play once that number hits the proverbial table.

The anchoring effect operates on the principle that the initial piece of information given, such as a salary figure, becomes the reference point for the rest of the negotiation. Regardless of its relevance, the initial anchor can sway perceptions and steer outcomes. For instance, if you propose a salary that's higher than the employer's expectation, it may expand the range of acceptable offers upward. Anchoring works like a psychological magnet, pulling parties closer to the anchor point. It's a strategic tool, turning the first number not into just a proposal but a pivot around which the entire negotiation revolves.

However, successfully using an anchor isn't about randomly throwing out a high number. It requires tact, preparation, and timing—a concept echoed throughout successful negotiation strategies. Before you walk into a negotiation room, know your worth. Researching your market value comprehensively helps in setting a suitable anchor. When the anchor is well-founded, it not only projects confidence but also rationalizes the figure in the eyes of your employer. This groundwork makes your offer appear logical and fair, thus increasing the odds of reaching a favorable agreement.

There's an art to presenting an anchor that resonates and persuades. Deliver your anchor with confidence and clarity. For instance, stating, "Based on my experience level and market research, I believe a salary of $85,000 is appropriate," sets a grounded tone. Providing this rationale simultaneously positions you as informed and reasonable. Such a statement is more compelling than a mere figure, and it shifts the conversation to evaluating the merits of your anchor rather than questioning its feasibility.

Employers, savvy to the anchoring effect, sometimes try to set their own anchors early in the conversation, often to your disadvantage. An employer might preemptively mention a low range to set expectations. Recognizing this tactic is crucial. Don't shy away from asserting your anchor if it aligns with your research and expectations. You can acknowledge their anchor while pivoting back to yours by saying, "I appreciate that range, though based on industry norms and my contributions, $85,000 feels aligned with my role's scope."

Timing, too, plays a significant role within the anchoring effect. Introducing your anchor too early might make you seem rigid, while too late might come off as indecisive. The ideal moment to state your anchor usually follows after laying groundwork; after demonstrating your value and understanding of the role. This sequence of sharing makes the transition to anchoring seamless, effortlessly positioning your figure as part of a larger, well-considered narrative.

Setting an appropriate anchor isn't only confined to salary figures. You can leverage anchors for other aspects of employment, such as perks, vacation days, or even benefits. By understanding the value of these components, you can anchor negotiations on total compensation rather than base salary alone, often opening paths to creative solutions and elevating overall satisfaction with the offer.

But what happens when you set an anchor and it's met with resistance or rejection? This is where flexibility in negotiation shines. Rather than regarding an anchor as a fixed point, consider it a part of a broader negotiation strategy. If the employer counters with a downward figure, evaluate it within the context of the entire offer. Use this as a moment to reassess other compensable aspects of the agreement. Remember, anchoring is more about focusing dialogue on your terms and ensuring any concessions are deliberate rather than hasty.

Anchoring can also be bolstered by anchoring-related techniques such as framing and priming. This might involve subtly leading up to your anchor by discussing past success stories or industry benchmarks that paint a picture of high value—yours. Frame these examples in a way that matches your narrative, subtly fortifying your anchor before it even enters the conversation.

In practice, mastering the anchoring effect requires experience and adaptability. Every negotiation offers lessons—some anchors may fail, while others open unexpected doors. Through practice, you'll refine your approach and develop a keen sense of when and how to anchor effectively, growing more adept with each negotiation you undertake. As you hone this skill, you'll find that you're not just aiming to set numbers but creating compelling narratives that navigate the negotiation to favorable outcomes.

Ultimately, anchoring is not about manipulation. It's about setting the stage for a balanced dialogue where both parties have a clear understanding of expectations and possibilities. By wielding this powerful psychological tool judiciously, you can transform your salary negotiations into a more equitable and successful exchange.

Utilizing Reciprocity to Your Advantage

Reciprocity is a powerful tool in human interaction, and its principles can be highly effective in salary negotiations. At its core, reciprocity operates on a simple yet profound idea: if you give something of value, there's an inherent expectation of receiving something in return. This principle rests on our deep-seated social instincts and can be strategically used to create favorable outcomes in negotiation scenarios.

To understand how reciprocity functions, consider a common experience: offering assistance to a colleague with a challenging project. Often, your act of generosity will result in the colleague feeling compelled to help you in the future. It's a cycle of give and take, built on mutual benefit and trust. Applying this principle in salary negotiations requires a nuanced approach, but when done effectively, it can significantly enhance your position.

One effective way to wield reciprocity in negotiations is by sharing valuable information that benefits the other party. By contributing insights or resources that assist your employer, you naturally position yourself as a valuable asset. This approach demonstrates your commitment not only to your role but also to the organization's success. In turn, it makes your request for higher compensation seem reasonable and deserving, positioning you for a successful negotiation.

Moreover, recognizing and responding to acts of reciprocity initiated by employers plays a crucial role. Employers may present their own offers—such as additional job responsibilities or development opportunities—as means to elevate your value. Acknowledging these gestures and reflecting similar appreciation can lead to a more constructive dialogue. When you engage in a reciprocal exchange, it opens avenues for discussing tangible benefits like salary adjustments.

Leveraging reciprocity isn't about coercion or manipulation; it's about fostering genuine relationships based on mutual respect and contribution. For example, by offering to take on an extra project or by participating in company initiatives that extend beyond your immediate responsibilities, you contribute to a culture of collaborative progress. When you later negotiate your salary, this history of mutual contribution can support your case for why your compensation should reflect your enhanced value.

It's also crucial to communicate how your contributions have positively impacted the organization. Narrative is a powerful ally in negotiations. Crafting your story around the times you've gone above and beyond can illustrate a pattern of reciprocal behavior. When you articulate how your actions have benefitted both your team and the broader company objectives, you reinforce your value proposition.

Understanding timing is essential when applying reciprocity in negotiations. Timing your reciprocation efforts to align with strategic moments—such as before a performance review or during budgeting season—can amplify their impact. When your contributions and goodwill are fresh in the employer's mind, your request for a salary increase is more likely to be well-received.

Interestingly, reciprocity goes beyond material contributions. It encompasses emotional and social elements. Expressing gratitude for opportunities provided by your employer can cultivate a positive ambiance that favors negotiation. A simple acknowledgment of past favor can smooth the path for future requests, reflecting a balanced give-and-take relationship.

Indeed, reciprocity can be a subtle dance in negotiations, requiring you to take calculated steps. It involves a blend of assertiveness and humility, ensuring you neither overstep what has been given nor undervalue your contributions. Approach negotiations with an openness to mutual benefit—offer suggestions on how both parties can gain from the arrangement. This openness epitomizes the essence of reciprocity, advancing your goals while recognizing your employer's needs.

However, it's important to be wary of overextending yourself in pursuit of reciprocity. Volunteering for every task with the hope of future rewards can lead to burnout and diminished returns. Instead, focus on select, strategic contributions that allow your efforts to be recognized and appreciated without compromising your well-being and productivity.

Evaluating each situation's dynamics will guide your reciprocity strategy. Every workplace and employer differs, and what might be effective in one context might not work in another. Cultivate an awareness of workplace culture and tailor your approach accordingly. Knowing what resonates with your employer—and what kind of contributions are genuinely valued—will enable you to leverage reciprocity effectively.

Ultimately, reciprocity offers a pathway to negotiate from a position of strength, where both parties are genuinely invested in each other's success. It fosters an environment where negotiation transforms from a transactional exchange to a partnership built on mutual benefit and shared goals. When executed with care and consideration, the principles of reciprocity don't just help you secure a higher salary; they position you as an invaluable contributor to your organization.

Chapter 9:
Framing Your Case

To truly command the salary you desire, constructing a persuasive narrative that underscores your unique value is paramount. It's about more than just listing accomplishments; it's about weaving these achievements into a compelling story that resonates with your employer's needs and goals. Begin by assessing your contributions and identifying how they align with the company's objectives, crafting your value into a pitch that is both confident and credible. Remember, this isn't merely about stating facts—it's about creating a vivid picture of how you drive success and why investing in you is a beneficial decision for the organization. Employ vivid examples, solid data, or testimonials where applicable, to leave an indelible impression that makes your ask not just reasonable, but necessary. By mastering this art of framing, you advocate not just for a number on your paycheck, but for a recognition of the integral role you play in the organization's journey.

Articulating Your Value

As we delve into the intricacies of salary negotiations, a crucial skill that stands out is articulating your value. It's not just about showcasing your achievements but strategically framing them in a way that aligns with your employer's needs and goals. At the heart of this lies an element of persuasion—an art that can transform an ordinary conversation into a compelling argument for your worth. In this chapter's journey, we'll unravel techniques that can sharpen your narrative and ensure your case is both heard and appreciated.

Understanding your value starts with self-reflection. To convey your worth effectively, you first need to internalize it. What unique skills do you bring to the table? How have your efforts led to tangible results? These are questions you need clear answers to. This self-awareness forms the backbone of your negotiation strategy. When you know your strengths and limitations, you can build a narrative that's honest yet compelling. It's essential to avoid overestimating or underselling yourself during this assessment.

Many people struggle with self-promotion, viewing it as boastful. But in reality, articulating your value isn't about bragging; it's about presenting facts and stories that highlight your contributions and expertise. Shifting this perspective can empower you to approach negotiations with more confidence. Consider the impact of framing your value as a dialogue rather than a monologue. Engage the employer in a conversation about your role in achieving common organizational goals.

Begin by mapping out specific accomplishments and framing them within the company context. Use quantitative data whenever possible—numbers don't lie and can make your achievements more concrete. For instance, instead of saying "I improved sales," you might say, "I increased sales by 20% through the implementation of a new marketing strategy." Such specifics provide clarity and leave a lasting impression, underscoring your direct impact on business outcomes.

It's also crucial to tailor your articulation to the audience. Each employer values different aspects based on industry, company culture, and current objectives. Conducting preliminary research into what matters most to the organization can guide which aspects of your value to highlight. A tech company might value your innovative problem-solving skills more than a retail company, which may be more interested in your ability to manage inventory efficiently under pressure.

Articulating your value effectively also demands you harness the power of storytelling. Humans are wired to respond to stories, making them an incredibly influential tool in negotiations. By structuring your accomplishments into a narrative, you can create a more engaging and memorable presentation of your value. Consider using a classic storytelling structure: setting the scene, establishing the challenge, highlighting your proactive approach, and concluding with the positive outcome.

Alongside stories, anticipate potential challenges or objections that might arise. Employers may question or downplay your contributions, intentionally or unintentionally. Prepare to counteract this by thinking ahead about likely pushbacks. For each key point, have a robust justification ready. Practice these rebuttals to maintain fluency in conversation, ensuring you don't get caught off guard during crucial moments.

Once you've articulated your value in this format, it's time to align it with future possibilities, showcasing your forward-looking value. Employers are interested in what you can continue to contribute. Enumerate how your skills and experiences position you to meet upcoming challenges or seize new opportunities within the organization. From developing new product lines to training teams in emerging technologies, paint a picture of continued growth and benefit.

The art of articulating your value doesn't end with what you say—how you say it matters tremendously. Your delivery, tone, and confidence play pivotal roles. Ensure your body language aligns with your words; maintain eye contact, practice active listening, and use open gestures. This conveys conviction and encourages receptiveness from the listener, reinforcing the impact of your words.

In addition to verbal communication, don't overlook the power of written documentation. A well-crafted email that reiterates your value points can serve as a reference for your manager or HR representative, particularly in larger organizations where negotiations may involve multiple stakeholders. An effective follow-up reinforces key messages and maintains momentum toward a favorable conclusion.

Timing also complements the art of articulation. Present your case at strategic moments—perhaps after a successful project completion or during performance reviews. These moments naturally lend themselves to discussions about your role and accomplishments. Moreover, when you're on the employer's radar for positive reasons, they might be more receptive to your pitch.

Ultimately, the key to articulating your value lies in preparation and delivery. Today's job market is highly competitive, and employers have countless options at their disposal. To stand out, you must present a finely polished case that's not only based on cold facts but also emotionally resonant and strategically aligned with the organization's vision. Mastering this skill turns a daunting task into an opportunity to pivot toward the salary and terms you deserve.

As you refine these techniques, remember that it's a dynamic process. Continuous improvement and adaptation enable you to articulate your value effectively, regardless of changing circumstances or roles. With practice, articulating your value becomes second nature, a lifeline in steering the course of your career negotiations with clarity and purpose.

Crafting the Perfect Pitch

The art of crafting the perfect pitch is pivotal when framing your case for salary negotiation. It's the moment when everything you've prepared comes together to articulate your worth and aspirations convincingly. This isn't just about compiling data or listing achievements; it's about telling your professional story in a compelling way that resonates with your employer's needs and values. A well-crafted pitch can tip the scales in your favor, setting the stage for a negotiation that's both successful and satisfying.

First, understand that your pitch is more than a sales pitch—it's an opportunity to align your goals with those of the organization. Begin by clearly defining what you want to achieve. Is it a salary increase, a new role, or additional responsibilities? Once you've established your goals, consider how they fit within the broader context of the company's objectives. This alignment is critical. Employers are more likely to respond positively if they see your goals as enhancing their mission. Therefore, your pitch should not only highlight your personal benefits but also underscore how these align with the company's success.

Narrative plays a crucial role in crafting your pitch. Begin by identifying your key achievements and contributions to the company. Quantify your successes with hard data whenever possible. Rather than simply stating that you improved efficiency, provide figures that illustrate the impact of your work. For example, explaining that you "increased department productivity by 20% over six months, resulting in significant cost savings" paints a vivid picture of your value.

Stories make data memorable and engaging. As you weave your narrative, incorporate anecdotes that highlight your problem-solving abilities, leadership skills, and adaptability. These stories should serve as evidence of your capabilities and readiness for the desired increase or role. They should reflect challenges you've overcome and lessons learned along the way. Personalize your pitch by drawing connections between your past achievements and future aspirations.

Persuasion forms the backbone of your pitch. To be effective, employ a mix of rational arguments and emotional appeals. Rationally, you need to substantiate your request with industry standards and market trends. Research the salaries for similar roles within your industry and region to support your numbers. Highlight how your performance aligns with or exceeds these benchmarks. On the emotional front, tapping into the power of storytelling can generate empathy and connect your employer to your journey. Explain why you are passionate about your role and how you're committed to the company's growth.

To reinforce your credibility, sprinkle in references to any continuous learning and professional development you've undertaken. Let your employer see that you are not just satisfied with resting on your laurels but are actively pursuing growth and improvement. This can include relevant certifications, online courses, or professional workshops you've attended. Such efforts demonstrate your dedication to evolving alongside the market and enhancing your contributions to the company.

Timing is another critical consideration in delivering your pitch. Pay attention to the organization's cycles and strategic planning periods. Is there a specific period when performance evaluations are conducted? Does the company have fiscal year budget planning sessions? Aligning your pitch with these timelines shows strategic thinking and respect for the company's processes.

Remember the power of preparation. Prior to your meeting, practice makes perfect. Engage in role-playing scenarios with a trusted mentor or colleague to hone your delivery. This practice can help you anticipate potential objections and refine your responses. Additionally, practicing in this way boosts your confidence, enabling you to present your pitch with poise and conviction. The more you rehearse, the better you'll perform under pressure.

Active listening is equally important during the negotiation itself. Once you've delivered your pitch, listen carefully to your employer's response. This will allow you to gauge their reaction and adjust your approach as necessary. Active listening involves being present in the conversation, showing empathy, and asking clarifying questions. This not only helps you understand their perspective but also demonstrates your willingness to collaborate towards a mutually beneficial outcome.

Flexibility should be a cornerstone of your strategy. While it's vital to have a clear goal, also be open to discussing alternative forms of compensation or adjustments to the role. Perhaps the budget doesn't allow for an immediate pay raise, but there could be room for additional benefits, flexible working conditions, or a future review. Showing willingness to explore these alternatives can differentiate you as not only a valuable employee but also a pragmatic negotiator.

Finally, conclude your pitch with a clear, actionable ask. After presenting your case and listening to input, succinctly state what you are hoping to gain from this conversation. This might be a specific number, a timeline for follow-up discussions, or agreement on performance milestones that would trigger future raises. Being direct and clear about your desired outcome leaves little room for ambiguity and ensures you are on the same page moving forward.

Framing your case effectively with a perfect pitch is an empowering process. It involves strategic preparation, compelling storytelling, and a nuanced understanding of timing and flexibility. As you hone these skills, you'll grow more adept at communicating the invaluable contributions you make to your team. In doing so, you'll increase your chances of securing not just the immediate improvements you seek, but also lay the groundwork for continued career advancement.

Chapter 10:
Handling Rejections

Facing rejection in salary negotiations can be disheartening, but it's an inevitable part of the process for anyone striving to boost their income. How you respond to a "no" can significantly shape future opportunities. The key is to maintain composure and stay engaged in the conversation. By treating rejection as an informative step rather than a setback, you pave the way for potential future discussions. Reflect on what might have contributed to the refusal and use resilient inquiry to understand the employer's perspective without sounding defensive. This insight can be invaluable for repositioning yourself and demonstrating your commitment to growth. Transforming a rejected raise into a chance for advancement involves a subtle blend of patience, optimism, and strategy. Seek feedback actively, express appreciation, and align your goals with the organization's long-term vision. This approach not only helps in sustaining a positive relationship with your employer but also sets the foundation for success in subsequent negotiations.

Responding to "No" with Grace

Hearing the word "no" during salary negotiations can feel like a personal setback. But it's crucial to remember that a rejection is not the end of the conversation. In fact, how you handle a "no" can significantly impact future interactions and your professional trajectory. Embracing this moment with composure and strategic thinking opens doors for future opportunities and fosters respect in the workplace.

First, let's talk about the initial reaction. It's natural to feel disappointed or even frustrated when faced with rejection. However, displaying emotional intelligence by controlling immediate reactions is key. Take a moment to breathe deeply and process the response before saying anything. This pause demonstrates maturity and gives you time to shift from an emotional to a more strategic mindset. It allows you to prepare for thoughtful engagement rather than an impulsive retort.

Acknowledging the decision with professionalism shows respect and opens the door for constructive dialogue. Respond with a simple acknowledgment, such as, "I understand. Thank you for considering my request." This response not only conveys humility but also sets the stage for further discussion. It reflects your professionalism and underscores your interest in finding a mutual understanding.

Once you've acknowledged the decision, it's beneficial to ask open-ended questions. These questions should aim to gather insights into the rejection and understand the employer's perspective. For example, you might ask, "Could you share more about how this decision was reached?" or "What are some areas I could focus on to strengthen my case for future opportunities?" Such questions demonstrate your willingness to grow and adapt, turning the conversation from a simple denial to a valuable learning opportunity.

It's also important to maintain a positive demeanor throughout the discussion. Gratitude is a powerful tool in salary negotiations. Thank your employer for their transparency and for the feedback they provide. Gratitude sets a positive tone and can soften the toughest of negotiations, helping in maintaining a strong professional relationship.

As the conversation progresses, it's valuable to express your continued enthusiasm for the role and organization. Affirm your commitment by stating how much you value your position and contributions to the company. This can be effectively communicated through statements like, "I appreciate the insights provided and am eager to continue contributing to our projects with improved vigor." This reassures your employer of your dedication, regardless of the outcome.

Moreover, make sure to use this interaction to gather information that will help you in future negotiations. Ask for specific feedback on performance metrics or company policy that influence salary adjustments. Understanding these factors will be critical in preparing for the next negotiation, allowing you to present a case that aligns more closely with the organization's goals or constraints.

Sometimes a "no" isn't set in stone but rather a "not now." Don't hesitate to ask about the possibility of revisiting the discussion in the near future. Inquire about setting a timeline for a performance review or a follow-up meeting. For instance, you might say, "Would it be possible to review my progress in the next six months with the aim of discussing this again?" This indicates your proactive approach toward career development and keeps the door open for future salary discussions.

If you're seeking growth, it might be beneficial to explore other forms of compensation or professional development opportunities. Use the opportunity to negotiate for additional benefits, like flexible work arrangements or professional development courses. Sometimes these components can be equally valuable in enhancing your career trajectory and overall job satisfaction.

Finally, reflect on the entire process after the negotiation. Analyze what went well and identify areas of improvement. Perhaps there was a misalignment between your expectations and the company's metrics, or maybe more preparation was needed. Every negotiation encounter is a learning experience, adding to your growth and refining your skills for future success.

All in all, handling a "no" with grace involves a combination of patience, strategic questioning, and a focus on long-term goals. With the right mindset, you transform an initial setback into a stepping stone toward achieving your desired career outcomes, maintaining respect, and fostering a trajectory bound for future success.

Turning a Denied Raise into Future Opportunities

Rejection, though initially discouraging, can be an invaluable stepping stone in the journey toward career advancement. When a raise is off the table, the resulting disappointment can feel like a hefty anchor. However, with the right mindset and approach, a denied raise doesn't have to spell the end. Instead, it's an opportunity to recalibrate your goals and set the stage for future success. Forging new paths from what appears to be a dead-end requires patience, a strategic reassessment, and possibly even a shift in perspective.

One of the first steps in transforming a rejection into a future opportunity is introspection and feedback. Consider scheduling a follow-up meeting with your supervisor to understand the reasons behind the denial. Use this as a chance to gather specific, constructive feedback. Questions like "What skills should I focus on developing?" or "What benchmarks do I need to hit to be considered for a future raise?" can yield actionable insights. This discussion not only clarifies your current standing but also demonstrates your engagement and commitment to growth. Moreover, it shows your employer that you're not satisfied with the status quo and are eager to evolve.

Once you have a clear understanding of your areas for improvement, it's time to craft a development plan. This plan should be concrete and measurable, outlining specific steps you will take to enhance your skills and value within the organization. Perhaps it's enrolling in a relevant course, volunteering for cross-departmental projects, or taking on new responsibilities that align with company objectives. Document these goals and the steps towards achieving them. This approach not only guides your progression but can also be shared with your manager to show that you're proactive and deliberate about your career trajectory.

Networking within and outside your company can also be a pivotal piece of the puzzle. Building robust professional relationships exposes you to new perspectives and opportunities. Seek mentorship or peer connections who can provide guidance, share knowledge, or even advocate on your behalf. Attend industry events or join relevant professional groups to expand your network beyond your current workplace. These connections can open doors to new challenges that stretch your capabilities and demonstrate your readiness for future responsibility.

Alongside personal development and networking, it's crucial to maintain a positive and resilient attitude. Perseverance in the face of rejection is a potent tool for long-term success. The road to a raise, much like any path to achieving significant goals, requires persistence. Setbacks might sting initially, but they can fortify your determination. Each "no" is not a permanent defeat but a temporary obstacle that equips you with the resilience needed to succeed in future negotiations. Your ability to bounce back reflects your potential for leadership and adaptability, qualities highly valued in any organization.

Another key strategy is to look beyond the raise itself and explore other avenues of professional growth within your role. Ask for additional responsibilities or projects that align with your career aspirations. These tasks can expand your skill set and showcase your ability to handle increased responsibility, positioning you for a raise later. They serve as tangible proof of your contributions and can strengthen your case during your next performance review. Furthermore, embracing new challenges can revitalize your engagement and satisfaction with your work, often leading to increased performance and recognition.

Consider also leveraging this moment to reassess your career goals. A denial prompts you to question whether your current path aligns with your long-term aspirations. It can be an opportunity to explore new interests or pivot to roles that may better utilize your skills or passions. Sometimes, a rejection is the nudge needed to make a transformational career decision that otherwise wouldn't have occurred. Align your current roles and responsibilities with where you ultimately want to be, ensuring every step you take is purposeful and conducive to your overarching career narrative.

Document your achievements and progress during this time diligently. Keeping track of projects completed, skills acquired, and milestones reached is not merely an exercise in self-congratulation. This detailed record will bolster your argument in future negotiations. When the next opportunity to request a raise arises, you'll be equipped with a well-documented narrative of your developmental journey and enhanced contributions, significantly strengthening your position.

Finally, it's essential to acknowledge and manage any emotional responses to rejection. While logic and strategy are critical, understanding and processing your emotions are just as important. Allow yourself to experience any initial disappointment but aim to quickly move into a productive mindset. Use techniques like mindfulness or journaling to regain focus and maintain your emotional well-being. Managing your emotions effectively enables you to adopt a composed, forward-looking attitude that will serve you well in future negotiations.

Remember, handling rejection gracefully and turning it into opportunity solidifies your reputation as a professional who isn't easily deterred. Your readiness to learn, adapt, and persevere reflects a growth mindset that can be a powerful differentiator in any field. While the immediate aftermath of a rejected raise can feel disheartening, it's an invitation for growth and exploration. By channeling disappointment into action, you're not only setting the stage for future raises but also carving a path to long-term career prosperity.

Chapter 11:
Developing Emotional Intelligence

In the fast-paced world of salary negotiations, developing emotional intelligence is a game-changer, equipping you with the ability to navigate conversations with both confidence and empathy. Emotional intelligence isn't just about keeping your stress in check—it's about understanding and managing your emotions while also tuning into the emotions of others. By honing this vital skill, you'll better manage the anxiety that can arise in high-stakes discussions, turning potential stressors into opportunities for connection and understanding. Mastering the art of reading emotional cues not only helps you anticipate the employer's responses but also allows you to respond in ways that build mutual respect and collaboration. This finesse can create an environment where both parties feel valued, boosting your chances of securing the salary you aim for. Emotional intelligence in negotiation isn't just a skill—it's a strategic advantage, paving the way for more effective and rewarding interactions.

Managing Anxiety and Stress

Negotiating for a better salary can stir up a mix of excitement and apprehension. These moments, ripe with opportunity, also bring emotional challenges. Anxiety and stress often rear their heads, influencing your negotiation strategies and outcomes. The good news is that by honing emotional intelligence, you can navigate these waters with more confidence and effectiveness.

At its core, emotional intelligence involves recognizing and managing our own emotions, as well as understanding and influencing the emotions of others. In the context of salary negotiation, this skill can be pivotal. When anxiety bubbles up, it can cloud judgment and hamper decision-making. Stress may lead to impulsively accepting an offer just to end the discomfort. To counter these effects, it's essential to develop techniques that foster both self-awareness and self-regulation.

Understanding the sources of anxiety is the first step. Salary discussions may trigger fears of inadequacy or concerns about conflict. You might worry about seeming greedy or alienating your employer. Recognizing these fears helps you address the root causes rather than just the symptoms. One effective approach is to reframe your perspective, viewing negotiation not as a confrontation, but as a collaboration toward mutually beneficial goals.

Preparation is another powerful antidote to stress. When you thoroughly research your market value and establish realistic salary goals, as discussed in earlier chapters, you lay a solid foundation of confidence. Confidence in your data and worth diminishes the unknowns, reducing anxiety. It's not just about having the facts but also about believing in your ability to convey them convincingly.

Practicing mindfulness can also play a significant role in managing stress. Techniques such as deep breathing, meditation, or even brief moments of reflection help clear your mind and center your thoughts. Before stepping into any negotiation, take a moment to engage in these practices. They prepare your mind for clarity and responsiveness rather than reactive behavior.

Role-playing scenarios, as previously explored, also aid in building resilience against stress. By simulating negotiation conversations, you familiarize yourself with the dynamics of dialogue and potential responses. This practice helps diminish anxiety by making the experience seem less foreign and intimidating. Each role-play session embeds a layer of familiarity, weaving comfort and competence into your negotiation toolkit.

The power of visualization should not be underestimated either. Visualizing a successful negotiation outcome can prime your mental state for success. As you imagine not just the details but the emotions involved in achieving your goals, your brain starts to align your actions toward realizing that vision. This practice can subtly lower anxiety and instill a positive outlook.

Another key aspect of managing anxiety and stress is maintaining a healthy work-life balance, even amidst crucial negotiations. Regular physical exercise, adequate sleep, and taking breaks to disconnect from work topics help sustain emotional resilience. A rested and fit mind handles pressure and adversities with more agility. Your physical wellness directly impacts your emotional state, influencing how you handle stress in negotiations.

Moreover, building a support network offers an invaluable buffer against anxiety. Whether it's mentors, peers, or professional groups, having people to discuss your aspirations and concerns with creates a platform for encouragement and advice. Conversations with people who've walked similar paths provide insights and foster a sense of solidarity, reducing feelings of isolation.

Lastly, developing coping mechanisms for when stress takes hold is crucial. Techniques such as cognitive restructuring allow you to challenge and change negative thought patterns. When you catch yourself thinking, "I'm not good enough for this salary," reframe it to, "I have the skills and experience that merit this pay." Consistently practicing these shifts in thinking patterns can rewire your responses to stressors, making them less daunting over time.

In conclusion, while anxiety and stress are natural companions in the salary negotiation process, they don't have to dictate the narrative.

By sharpening your emotional intelligence and adopting comprehensive strategies for emotional management, you can transform these challenges into stepping stones. Each encounter strengthens your resolve, reinforcing your path toward negotiating with confidence and achieving the pay you deserve.

Reading Emotional Cues

Negotiating a salary is as much an interpersonal dance as it is a tactical exercise. At its core, it involves a sophisticated layer of emotional dynamics that can significantly sway the outcome. By honing the ability to read emotional cues, you can tap into an often-overlooked element of negotiation—empathy. Being able to gauge the emotions of the other party allows for a more nuanced and effective approach, transforming a potentially adversarial interaction into a collaborative dialogue. Indeed, recognizing and appropriately responding to these cues can make the difference between a stalled negotiation and a successful outcome.

To understand emotional cues, one must first be attuned to the non-verbal signs that people often exhibit unconsciously. These include facial expressions, body language, and tone of voice—each a window into the thoughts and feelings that aren't always articulated. For instance, crossed arms could indicate defensiveness or discomfort, while a nod could convey agreement or understanding. Similarly, a shift in tone, whether it turns warmer or terser, can signal either receptivity to your propositions or resistance. Appreciating these subtleties equips you with the tools to adapt your strategy dynamically throughout the negotiation process.

It's crucial to remember that emotional cues aren't just detected in others; they're also communicated by you. Self-awareness plays a critical role in ensuring that the signals you send match your intended message. An incongruence between your words and your emotional cues can confuse the recipient and undermine your credibility. Therefore, practicing control over your own expressions and physical demeanor allows for smoother interactions. Regularly reflecting on and adjusting your own body language, such as maintaining eye contact and an open stance, fosters an environment of trust and sincerity.

Moreover, emotional cues are not isolated to face-to-face interactions. In today's diverse professional landscape, virtual negotiations are increasingly common. Here, reading emotional cues requires paying close attention to intonations, pauses, and the pacing of speech. Without visual cues available in a digital setting, these auditory signals become even more critical. The lack of physical presence demands that negotiators be especially perceptive, finely attuning their listening skills to pick up on any underlying emotions that might not be directly expressed.

Empathy, the ability to understand and share the feelings of another, becomes pivotal in this context. By striving to see the world through the eyes of your counterpart, you forge a deeper connection and can anticipate potential objections. Empathic engagement doesn't mean sacrificing your own needs; rather, it helps in identifying mutual interests and crafting solutions that respect both parties. Cultivating empathy involves both a mindset shift and a skill development component, honed through active listening and open-ended questioning during negotiation dialogues.

Developing an awareness of your own emotional state is equally important. Emotions are powerful forces that can steer the course of a negotiation, often unpredictably. Recognizing when you're feeling anxious or frustrated allows you to take deliberate actions to manage these emotions before they manifest unconsciously as negative cues. Conscious regulation, such as taking a moment to breathe deeply or reframing your outlook mid-conversation, can provide clarity and poise, allowing you to maintain a calm disposition and make strategic decisions despite emotional provocations.

Curiously, being attuned to another's emotional state can also involve employing patience. Negotiations can be tense, with parties sometimes caught in the throes of emotional responses that require time to subside. Creating space for the other party to express and work through their feelings can often turn a fraught situation around. This patience signals to your counterpart that you value the relationship and that you're considerate of their emotions, which can soften their stance and open up room for collaboration.

Feedback mechanisms also play a valuable role in refining how we read and respond to emotional cues. After negotiations, reflecting on interactions and seeking input from trusted colleagues can highlight areas for growth. Perhaps there was a moment when a point didn't land as expected or an opportunity to connect emotionally was missed. Constructive feedback helps illuminate blind spots and fortifies future readiness by reinforcing effective strategies and mitigating common errors. Moreover, this process affirms the iterative nature of developing emotional intelligence.

Over time, integrating the awareness of emotional dynamics into your negotiation repertoire enhances your ability to navigate complex, multi-layered negotiation scenarios confidently. It empowers you to remain agile and responsive, tailoring your approach to align with the evolving emotional landscape of each negotiation. Earning the trust and respect of your negotiating partners—even in moments of disagreement—becomes a strategic edge in achieving your desired outcomes.

In essence, mastering the reading of emotional cues isn't simply about achieving a narrow win in any one negotiation. It's about cultivating a skill set that elevates your career over the long term. Through improved relationships and a robust reputation as a mindful and considerate negotiator, opportunities for advancement and salary growth become more accessible. By investing in the development of your emotional intelligence, you build a resilient foundation that supports both personal and professional success in every negotiation you encounter.

Chapter 12:
Gender and Salary Negotiation

Negotiating salaries can be a daunting task, particularly when gender dynamics come into play, yet understanding and leveraging these dynamics can transform challenges into opportunities. Research has consistently shown that gender bias impacts salary negotiations, but awareness of this bias is the first step towards overcoming it. Women, who historically face more pushback and skepticism when negotiating salaries, can benefit from embracing strategies that empower and assert their value. It's crucial to shift societal perceptions that still cling to outdated notions of gender roles in the workplace by confidently articulating individual worth and accomplishments during negotiations. By preparing thoroughly, understanding personal market value, and framing negotiations with a focus on collective benefits rather than personal gain, women can enhance the chances of successful outcomes. Additionally, fostering alliances and seeking mentorship can provide the necessary support and encouragement to counteract gender-related obstacles, making it clear that these negotiations are not just about personal success, but about paving the path for more equitable workplaces for everyone. Empowerment in salary negotiations doesn't just serve individual pursuits; it contributes to a broader narrative of gender equality in professional environments.

Addressing Gender Bias

The landscape of salary negotiation is an intricate tapestry, woven with threads of psychology, strategy, and societal norms. At the core lies an enduring challenge: gender bias. Tackling this issue requires unraveling long-standing biases and empowering individuals to navigate them with resilience and confidence. Gender bias in salary negotiation is not just a women's issue; it's a societal one, trickling down to affect organizational success and economic growth. The stakes are high, demanding informed strategies and concerted efforts.

Understanding gender bias begins with recognizing its presence in the negotiation process. Often, women face a societal expectation to be accommodating and collaborative, which can influence both their approach and how their negotiations are received. This ingrained perception can lead to outcomes where assertiveness in women is viewed negatively, whereas the same traits might be celebrated in men. Such biases are not always overt, making them particularly insidious and difficult to counteract without deliberate strategy.

One effective approach in addressing gender bias is fostering an awareness of these biases among everyone involved in negotiations. Negotiation education should include training on unconscious biases and their impact on decision-making. Companies can play a pivotal role by incorporating bias training into their HR practices, ensuring that hiring and salary decisions are based on merit and not influenced by gender-stereotypical perceptions.

For individuals, it's crucial to come prepared with concrete data that highlights their market value. This empowers them to base conversations on facts and credentials rather than subjective assessments that might be clouded by bias. Women, in particular, can benefit from benchmarking their salary expectations based on industry standards and peer comparisons. This framework transforms the negotiation into a discussion of value and contribution, steering it away from personal traits.

Moreover, storytelling is a powerful tool in addressing gender bias. Articulating one's achievements through narrative can humanize the negotiation, showcasing the impact of past contributions and future potential. Reframing the negotiation discourse to focus on outcomes and contributions helps in bypassing biases that might be rooted in gender stereotypes.

Mentorship and sponsorship are invaluable in combating gender bias. Creating opportunities for mentorship allows more experienced negotiators to share insights and strategies, empowering women to approach negotiations with greater confidence. Sponsors, on the other hand, actively advocate for their proteges, helping to offset biases by validating the individual's professional worth within their networks.

Flexibility in negotiation can also mitigate gender bias by broadening the scope of what is considered negotiable. Exploring a mix of salary and other benefits like flexible working hours, additional vacation time, or professional development opportunities can appeal to a diverse set of needs and reduce the impact of potential biases in salary alone.

Addressing gender bias also demands institutional changes. Organizations should establish transparent processes for salary and promotion decisions, making clear the criteria and benchmarks used. This transparency can diminish opportunities for bias, as decisions are openly tied to quantifiable and standardized criteria.

The promotion of an inclusive culture that values diverse leadership styles is essential to dismantling bias. Companies that embrace a multitude of perspectives and approaches can foster an environment where all employees feel valued for their unique contributions, rather than being boxed into traditional gender roles.

Ultimately, tackling gender bias in salary negotiations requires a multifaceted approach that involves individual preparation and broader societal change. By acknowledging the issue and taking systematic steps to address it, both individuals and organizations can move towards a future where salary negotiation is truly based on merit, value, and potential.

Progress will take time, but with the right strategies, we can break down the barriers of gender bias and pave the way for equitable salary negotiations. Let's commit to ongoing dialogue, education, and action to ensure that future generations engage in negotiations devoid of gender-based constraints.

Empowering Women in Negotiations

When it comes to salary negotiations, women have historically faced unique challenges that stem from cultural, social, and institutional biases. These barriers often result in women being underpaid compared to their male counterparts, even when experience and qualifications are similar. However, by recognizing these challenges and empowering women with targeted strategies and support, it's possible to level the playing field and ensure fair compensation.

Understanding the landscape of gender and salary negotiation requires an acknowledgment of the broader systemic issues at play. Numerous studies suggest that women are less likely to initiate salary negotiations. This hesitation often springs from societal norms that can label assertive women as aggressive, a double standard not typically applied to men. The fear of negative repercussions or being judged can lead women to avoid negotiations altogether. Recognizing these ingrained biases is the first step toward empowerment.

One pivotal strategy to empower women in negotiations is through education and self-awareness. Women should be encouraged to understand their worth in the job market. This can be achieved by conducting thorough research on salary data within their industry and role. Knowing the average salaries helps women benchmark their expectations and feel more confident in their negotiations. It's crucial that they enter discussions armed with facts and figures to bolster their case.

Moreover, confidence-building is essential. Psychological research underscores the importance of believing in one's value and capabilities. Women need to cultivate a mindset that doesn't shy away from tough conversations. Confidence can be nurtured through various methods, including practicing negotiations in safe environments. Role-playing with friends or mentors can simulate real-world scenarios, helping women prepare responses to potential objections.

Developing effective communication skills is another key component. Articulating one's contributions and future potential convincingly can sway negotiation outcomes. Women should focus on framing their discussions around their achievements and the value they bring to the organization. This narrative helps shift the perception from personal needs to the benefits they offer the company. Additionally, practicing active listening during negotiations can provide useful insights into employers' viewpoints, allowing women to address concerns more precisely.

Timing and strategy are also critical factors. Women should be strategic about when they choose to negotiate. Evaluating organizational moments — such as after a successful project or during the company's financially strong periods — can create additional leverage. Synchronizing personal achievements with company successes can make it harder for employers to deny a raise.

Another empowering approach is understanding and countering employer tactics. By recognizing common negotiation strategies used by employers, women can better prepare to respond. For instance, if an employer starts with a lowball offer, women should not settle; instead, they can use this as a base to negotiate upwards. It's crucial to remain firm yet flexible throughout the process.

Psychological principles such as anchoring and reciprocity can be particularly useful. Anchoring refers to setting a target higher than what's expected, which can influence final outcomes in one's favor. Reciprocity involves building a negotiation atmosphere based on mutual respect and exchange, which can foster positive outcomes for both parties. These techniques can empower women to steer discussions more effectively and achieve favorable terms.

Handling rejections with grace is another skill women must hone. Inevitably, not all negotiation attempts will end in success. However, receiving a "no" shouldn't be disheartening. Instead, it can be an opportunity to seek feedback and express a willingness to revisit the conversation in the future. Constructive dialogue after a rejection can leave the door open for future negotiations.

Developing emotional intelligence plays a fundamental role in empowering women in salary discussions. Understanding and managing one's emotions reduce anxiety and stress, which are common in high-stakes conversations. By maintaining composure, women can present their case more clearly and calmly, ensuring their points are heard and respected.

Support systems can also amplify women's negotiation successes. Networking with other women professionals and seeking guidance from mentors who've successfully navigated similar challenges can provide valuable insights and encouragement. Sharing experiences and strategies can demystify the negotiation process, making it less daunting.

In addition, organizations have a role to play in empowering women within their workforce. They can facilitate workshops on negotiation skills and equitable pay, fostering an inclusive cultural environment where women feel comfortable and justified in negotiating their salary. By promoting transparency in pay structures and establishing mentorship programs, companies can contribute significantly to the empowerment of women.

Finally, empowering women involves not just individual efforts but also collective action. Advocacy for policy changes that address gender-based discrepancies in compensation structures is crucial. Efforts to bridge the gender pay gap must be relentless, as they affect not just individual women, but society as a whole.

Empowering women in negotiations is a multifaceted endeavor that requires both personal initiative and systemic change. By educating, building confidence, and leveraging psychological strategies, women can become more assertive and successful in their negotiation efforts. In turn, this empowerment leads not only to better compensation but also to increased representation and influence in workplaces worldwide.

Chapter 13:
Cultural Considerations

In today's interconnected world, mastering salary negotiations requires more than just understanding the basics; it demands a sensitivity to cultural nuances that can shape the entire dialogue. Whether you're negotiating domestically or with international stakeholders, recognizing how cultural norms influence perceptions of authority, communication styles, and decision-making processes is crucial. Every culture has its own set of expectations, and adapting your negotiation strategy accordingly can turn challenges into opportunities. By valuing diverse perspectives and listening actively, you can navigate complex cross-cultural landscapes with confidence. Embrace adaptability, as it's your ally in building bridges and crafting solutions that resonate globally. Remember, cultural awareness isn't just about avoiding missteps—it's about enriching your negotiation approach with empathy and wisdom, ultimately paving the way for more meaningful and successful outcomes across borders.

Navigating Cross-Cultural Negotiations

In today's globally connected world, it's common for salary negotiations to cross international and cultural boundaries. The ability to navigate cross-cultural negotiations is a vital skill for professionals seeking to maximize their compensation. This section will provide insights into the cultural nuances that can influence negotiation strategies, enabling you to approach such discussions with confidence and respect.

Negotiating across cultures presents unique challenges, but it also offers opportunities for significant learning and growth. Understanding cultural differences and their impact on communication can transform a potentially intimidating process into a constructive dialogue. Each culture has its own set of norms and expectations, which can influence how negotiations are conducted, what is considered polite or aggressive, and the pace at which negotiations proceed.

Consider the importance of context in communication. In some cultures, such as those in high-context societies like Japan or China, much is communicated through context rather than direct words. This means that body language, tone of voice, and even silence carry significant weight. In contrast, low-context cultures, like the United States or Germany, rely more on explicit verbal communication, where words convey the primary message. Recognizing these differences allows you to adjust your negotiation style accordingly, ensuring that you interpret signals correctly and convey your intentions clearly.

Respect and relationships are often prioritized over business outcomes in numerous cultures. For example, in many Middle Eastern and Latin American countries, establishing a personal rapport is critical before delving into negotiations. This approach contrasts with Western cultures that may focus immediately on the task at hand. Building relationships can be time-consuming, but investing in this process can lead to more fruitful negotiations. Taking the time to understand and honor these relationship-driven perspectives can differentiate you as a negotiator who is respectful and well-prepared.

Time perception also varies across cultures and can significantly impact negotiations. In cultures where time is perceived linearly, such as in the United States, punctuality and time management are imperative. Conversely, in cultures where time is more flexible, like many in Africa or the Middle East, negotiations may not adhere to strict schedules. Being patient and adaptable to these cultural perceptions of time can demonstrate respect and enhance mutual understanding.

Hierarchy and authority play a role in negotiation dynamics as well. In cultures with high power distance, such as in many Asian and Middle Eastern countries, authority figures are often given great deference. Negotiators must respect these hierarchies and understand how they affect decision-making processes. On the other hand, cultures with low power distance, like Scandinavian countries, may encourage more egalitarian discussions where all parties are viewed as equals. Understanding these differing approaches to hierarchy will influence who you negotiate with and how you address them.

When approaching cross-cultural salary negotiations, it's essential to do your homework. Research cultural norms, values, and business etiquette related to the country or culture you are engaging with. This preparation demonstrates a commitment to understanding and respect, building trust even before the negotiation begins. Utilize resources such as international business guides or cultural consultants to supplement your knowledge.

In practical terms, cultural awareness affects not just the communication style but also the structure and content of the negotiation itself. Consider the importance of seniority in your negotiation team: should you include senior colleagues to match the expectations of your counterparts? Are certain negotiation topics sensitive or taboo in the culture you are negotiating with? Understanding these elements can prevent missteps and position you as a thoughtful negotiator.

Entering negotiations with cultural intelligence means recognizing that while cultural norms inform behavior, individuals may not adhere strictly to these norms. There's always room for personal differences, and being attuned to this can help avoid stereotyping or assuming there's a one-size-fits-all approach within a culture. Flexibility and adaptability are your allies in cross-cultural negotiation situations.

Effective cross-cultural negotiation also relies heavily on listening—a crucial skill that's universally applicable. Active listening goes beyond just hearing words; it involves paying attention to non-verbal cues, seeking to understand the emotions and motivations of others, and validating the other party's perspective. This fosters a collaborative atmosphere conducive to mutual gain, an outcome that is as rewarding as it is sustainable.

Moreover, when language barriers present challenges, investing in a competent translator or interpreter can be invaluable. These professionals ensure clear communication and can provide cultural insights, helping bridge any gaps that could create misunderstanding or tension. Remember, in any negotiation, clarity is power.

Finally, adopting a mindset of curiosity and openness can remarkably influence the outcome of cross-cultural negotiations. Approaching each interaction with a willingness to learn and a respect for diversity allows for enriched experiences and potentially more innovative solutions. This attitude also helps in mitigating the biases that can cloud judgment and impede negotiations.

In essence, the key to successful cross-cultural negotiations lies in preparation, empathy, and a genuine respect for diversity. By understanding and appreciating the cultural dimensions of negotiation, you position yourself to not only secure a favorable agreement but also cultivate lasting professional relationships. Such skills are not merely valuable in salary negotiation but extend to all aspects of global business interactions, enriching your career and personal growth journey.

Adapting Strategies for Global Contexts

In today's interconnected world, salary negotiation isn't confined to one's own cultural backyard. As enterprises expand, increasingly, negotiations cross geographical boundaries and cultural lines. If you're looking to negotiate on a global scale, understanding how to adapt your strategies to various cultural contexts becomes crucial. What might work seamlessly in one part of the world could fall flat or even offend in another. Adapting your strategy doesn't mean losing your edge; instead, it's about becoming more effective and nuanced in your approach.

Different cultures have unique approaches to communication, often shaped by deep-rooted values and societal norms. For example, while some cultures favor a direct style of negotiation, others may perceive it as too aggressive. When negotiating salaries globally, it's important to be cognizant of how the cultural backdrop can influence both the process and the outcome. It's not just about the words you use, but also the nonverbal cues, the context, and the pacing of your negotiation.

Take, for instance, the concept of silence during a negotiation. In many Western cultures, silence might be seen as awkward, or even as a sign of weakness. Conversely, in some Asian cultures, silence can be a strategic tool, providing space for reflection and indicating respect for the process. By understanding these subtleties, you can more effectively craft your strategy to align with the cultural norms and expectations of the person across the table.

Flexibility is key when adapting strategies for a global context. Rigidly adhering to one style or set of tactics can leave you vulnerable to missteps. In many cultures, building relationships is seen as paramount and can influence the negotiation outcomes significantly. This often means that the negotiation process may take longer, with a greater emphasis on informal discussions and trust-building exercises prior to getting down to the business of numbers and figures.

Moreover, understanding and respecting cultural hierarchies can also impact your negotiation success. In cultures where hierarchy and respect for authority are highly valued, your ability to recognize and navigate these dynamics will shape how your negotiation unfolds. Acknowledging the decision-making process and who holds the power can help you tailor your strategy and ensure a more respectful and effective communication approach.

Cultural empathy stands as a pillar in global negotiations. It's not merely about recognizing differences, but truly appreciating and valuing them. When entering negotiations in a global context, take the time to learn about the other party's cultural background and how this may influence their negotiation style and expectations. This awareness not only aids in formulating your approach but also demonstrates respect for the diversity of perspectives.

Language, a powerful tool in negotiation, can be both a bridge and a barrier. Even when a common language is spoken, nuances and idiomatic expressions may be lost in translation. To overcome this, clarity, simplicity, and sometimes professional translation services can prevent misunderstandings. It's often helpful to repeat and confirm key points throughout the negotiation to ensure both parties are aligned and any potential ambiguities are clarified.

A successful negotiation strategy in a global context is not just about what you bring to the table, but how you bring it. For instance, while American negotiations often involve assertiveness and a focus on individual accomplishments, other cultures may value consensus and collective achievements. Recognizing when to adjust your approach from an individualistic to a collectivistic one can significantly influence how your proposals are received and evaluated.

Another aspect of global salary negotiations is adapting to the varied legal and regulatory frameworks across different countries. Each region may have its own set of rules regarding employment agreements, tax implications, and salary regulations. It's imperative to equip yourself with this knowledge to ensure that your negotiation strategy is not only culturally appropriate but also compliant with local laws and practices. Engaging a local expert or seeking legal advice can provide invaluable insights.

When considering gender roles and expectations, be aware that these too vary widely across cultures and can affect negotiation dynamics. In some cultures, there may be predetermined expectations about gender roles within professional settings, which can influence both the negotiation process and the outcomes. By being aware of these cultural variances, you can better prepare to either navigate or leverage them in a way that aligns with your negotiation goals.

Successful global negotiators also appreciate the value of patience and the long-term approach. In some markets, sealing the deal is not just about immediate gains but forming a sustainable relationship that yields benefits over time. This often requires a delicate balance between reaching a satisfactory agreement today, while investing in a relationship that may open doors to further opportunities in the future.

The digital age has facilitated cross-cultural negotiations by making tools for communication more accessible. Regardless of geographical boundaries, leveraging technology can aid in understanding cultural nuances better than ever. Whether through virtual meetings or online resources that provide cultural insights, you now have myriad tools at your disposal to fine-tune your approach before stepping into a negotiation.

In conclusion, adapting salary negotiation strategies for global contexts requires both sensitivity to cultural differences and a strategic approach that respects these distinctions. It's about blending the art of negotiation with the science of cultural understanding. By approaching each negotiation with a mindset that embraces diversity and adaptability, you enhance your capacity to achieve mutually beneficial outcomes, setting a foundation not only for successful negotiations but for lasting professional relationships across the globe. Embrace the global tapestry of negotiations and let it enrich both your skills and your career journey.

Chapter 14:
Negotiation in Remote
Work Environments

In today's increasingly digital world, mastering negotiation in remote work environments has become an essential skill. As virtual communication platforms become the norm, the traditional dynamics of salary negotiation are evolving, requiring a fresh approach to demonstrate value effectively. Engaging with employers or clients remotely demands impeccable clarity and consistency in communication. Be it through video calls, emails, or virtual collaborative tools, maintaining a persuasive presence requires adapting age-old techniques to meet the demands of these digital landscapes. It's about embracing the flexibility of these platforms to not only articulate one's worth with confidence but also to listen actively and steer the conversation towards a mutually beneficial outcome. As you navigate these virtual waters, remember that each interaction is an opportunity to establish rapport and build lasting professional relationships, which are as crucial in remote settings as they are in person. Your ability to negotiate successfully in remote work environments hinges on the seamless integration of strategic thinking, emotional intelligence, and effective use of technology, laying the groundwork for securing the compensation you deserve.

Adapting to Virtual Negotiation Settings

The shift to remote work has dramatically altered how we negotiate salaries. Where once face-to-face conversations ruled, now our discussions happen over video calls or emails. This shift requires a different set of skills and an adaptable mindset. To excel in virtual negotiations, understanding the nuances of digital communication is crucial. You can't rely on handshakes and physical presence anymore. Instead, you need to harness the virtual space to your advantage, developing new ways to express confidence and articulate your value.

First, let's talk about establishing a strong virtual presence. The screen separates you from the person you're negotiating with, making it harder to convey the nuances that come with in-person interactions. So, pay attention to your on-screen appearance. Dress the part, just as you would for an in-office meeting. Position your camera at eye level and ensure adequate lighting. A clutter-free background can also help maintain focus. The clearer and more professional you appear, the better you'll connect. These visual cues, while subtle, build the perception of professionalism and competence.

Now, consider the technology itself. Familiarity with the platform you are using is non-negotiable. Whether it's Zoom, Skype, or Microsoft Teams, each has its features and quirks. Knowing these in advance can prevent tech hiccups that might disrupt the negotiation flow. Test your equipment—microphone, camera, and internet connection—beforehand to ensure everything works smoothly. Being proactive about these factors sets a solid foundation, underscoring your preparation and attention to detail.

One of the greatest challenges in virtual settings is the absence of physical cues, like body language, that convey trust and intent. This means you need to place extra emphasis on vocal elements—tone, pace, and inflection—to mirror the effect these cues would have. Speak clearly and deliberately, making sure that your enthusiasm and confidence resonate through your voice. Silences can seem more pronounced virtually, so don't be afraid to embrace a pause. They give both you and your counterpart time to think and reflect, often encouraging a more thoughtful exchange.

Active listening takes on a new dimension here, too. You might be tempted to glance at notes or multi-task, but maintaining eye contact (or at least the appearance of it) and nodding affirmatively can go a long way in showing your engagement. Remember, you're not just hearing the words—you're interpreting their meaning. Acknowledging your negotiation partner's points, and strategically using verbal affirmations like "I understand" or "That's a good point," can strengthen your position.

Another important element is the timing of your negotiations. Remote work environments often blur personal and work boundaries, making it crucial to set a time that is most convenient and least stressful. Avoid scheduling negotiations during heavy workload periods or when distractions might arise. Find mutually agreeable times, showing respect for both parties' time zones and commitments. A well-chosen time enhances focus and shows your respect for their schedule, which can positively influence their receptivity to your proposals.

Importantly, virtual negotiations often require additional materials to support your case, which can be an advantage if used correctly. You can share documents, presentations, or data in real-time that bolster your salary request. Ensure these resources are well-prepared and, ideally, shared ahead of the meeting. This preparation not only supports your argument but also demonstrates professionalism and thoroughness. Craft these materials to be clear and concise, enabling your counterpart to see the value you bring without distraction or ambiguity.

Moreover, understanding and deploying psychological tools remain relevant in virtual settings. Techniques like anchoring still apply. Introducing your salary expectations confidently and early in the discussion can subtly shape the direction of the negotiation. Observe how your counterpart reacts to these anchors. Their response might not be as visibly immediate as it would be face-to-face, but tone changes or slight hesitations can be telling. Use these cues to steer the conversation advantageously.

Finally, remember that patience and resilience are key. Negotiations might take longer in virtual formats due to delays in communication and the time required to digest information without the immediate feedback of in-person meetings. If your initial request isn't met with enthusiasm, don't rush to conclusions. Follow up with thoughtful questions, and reiterate your value gently but assertively. Show you're flexible but firm, open to finding mutual benefit. Each interaction is an opportunity to refine your technique and approach.

Virtual negotiation calls for embracing the medium's strengths while mitigating its challenges. By honing your digital communication skills, maintaining professional decorum, and leveraging psychological insights, you'll navigate these settings with confidence and poise. The goal is to ensure your value shines through, regardless of the format. As work environments continue to adapt, so must our negotiation practices, ensuring that distance never diminishes our capacity to advocate for ourselves effectively. Ultimately, mastering the virtual landscape opens new possibilities, empowering you to achieve the salary outcome you deserve in today's ever-evolving workplace.

Communicating Value Remotely

In a world where remote work is increasingly becoming the norm, negotiating effectively from behind a computer screen is a vital skill. Communicating your value remotely can feel daunting, given the lack of physical presence and the nuances of in-person interactions. Yet, mastering this skill goes beyond mere adaptation; it's about embracing new communication modalities and understanding how to use them to your advantage. It involves being intentional and strategic in conveying your worth to potential or current employers. Remember, expressing your value is not just about stating your qualifications but also about how you contribute uniquely to the organization's success.

Remote work may strip away some traditional negotiation tools, like non-verbal cues or a firm handshake, but it also equips you with technological advancements that can be leveraged to present your case more effectively. With thoughtfully crafted emails or virtual presentations, you can communicate the same enthusiasm and professionalism as you would in face-to-face meetings. In fact, the digital age offers creative ways to demonstrate your contributions through visual aids, data analytics, and strategic documents, all aimed at strengthening your position. It's essential to harness these tools and articulate your value compellingly.

To effectively communicate your value remotely, start by preparing thoroughly. This involves understanding the organization's goals and articulating how your skills, experiences, and achievements align with them. Translate your accomplishments into a quantifiable format—numbers and data can be particularly persuasive, as they provide concrete evidence of your contributions. For instance, "Increased website traffic by 50% through strategic content development" holds much more weight than a vague assertion of having "improved digital engagement." When you clearly connect your work results to the company's needs, your value proposition becomes evident and irrefutable.

Consider your role through the lens of impact, rather than mere job duty fulfillment. In many cases, remote work can obscure the tangible differences employees make to their teams or projects. By framing your experiences around the benefits and transformations you've facilitated, rather than just listing your responsibilities, you drastically differentiate your narrative. This approach not only showcases your past performances but also sets a precedent for future potential. As you prepare, think critically about situations where you exhibited leadership, solved problems proactively, or contributed to team success, regardless of whether these were documented in your job description.

Communication, especially in a remote setting, is rarely just verbal. Written communication—emails, messages, reports—plays a critical role in how your value is perceived. It's crucial to maintain clarity and conciseness while avoiding overly technical jargon that might detract from your message. Equally important is your ability to listen actively to feedback and questions. This form of effective communication demonstrates respect and a willingness to engage—two essential traits that paint you as a valuable, collaborative team member. Pay attention to your tone; it affects how your message is received. While working remotely removes non-verbal cues, your choice of words and organization of thoughts often carry the weight in conveying professionalism and competence.

Another critical strategy is cultivating relationships within your virtual workspace. Networking doesn't automatically translate from in-person to online environments, but it's no less important. Schedule regular one-on-ones or group discussions with colleagues and supervisors to exchange ideas, gain insights, and demonstrate your knowledge and expertise. Offering help on projects outside your immediate responsibilities can also prove your capabilities in diverse contexts, further cementing your value within the organization. Over time, such involvement can strengthen your collateral when negotiating, as you have built a network of allies who support and recognize your contributions.

When the time comes to negotiate, leverage technology to your advantage. Tools like video conferencing can allow you to create a more personal interaction, where you can express your enthusiasm and strategically emphasize points using visual aids. This modality also allows for a transparent discussion, as you are operating from a location of your choice, where comfort can breed confidence. Ensure your environment is free from distractions, reinforcing your professionalism and focus. Despite the physical distance, your active engagement during these negotiations signals dedication and commitment to the role.

Don't underestimate the power of a well-timed communication plan. An effective presentation of your value is about more than what you say—timing and approach can significantly affect outcomes. Introduce your achievements and anticipated contributions at strategic moments, such as during project reviews or quarterly assessments. These contexts amplify the relevance of your work to the organization's overarching goals, positioning your value in parallel with the company's vision. Demonstrating an acute understanding of the timing and organizational strategy highlights your competence and alignment with business objectives.

While remote work necessitates adaptation, it also offers opportunities that shouldn't be overlooked. You bring the skills, achievements, and perspectives that can add tangible value to any organization. By sharpening your ability to communicate these elements effectively, you not only enhance your negotiation outcomes but also advance your career in a digitally connected world. Embrace the challenge and leverage the tools at your disposal to turn virtual limitations into new avenues for expressing your worth. Remember, effectively communicating your value remotely is not just about adapting to a changing work environment; it's about pioneering new norms for professional success in the digital era.

Chapter 15:
Using Technology to Your Advantage

In today's digital age, technology isn't just a tool—it's a powerful ally in your salary negotiation arsenal. Embracing digital platforms can open doors to invaluable resources that bolster your research and preparation, giving you a competitive edge. With tools like salary calculators and industry reports at your fingertips, you can craft a compelling case rooted in data, not guesswork. But it's not just about crunching numbers; technology enhances communication too. Virtual meeting software and professional networking sites allow you to articulate your value with precision and poise, even if you're negotiating from miles away. By integrating technology seamlessly into your strategy, you can articulate your worth confidently and push for that well-deserved increase. It's about leveraging all available tools to not just meet expectations, but exceed them, turning aspirations into tangible outcomes.

Tools for Research and Preparation

The success of any negotiation heavily relies on thorough research and impeccable preparation. Before stepping into salary discussions, it's crucial to arm yourself with the right information and tools. In this digital age, technology offers a wealth of resources that can empower you to feel more confident, informed, and ready to tackle even the toughest of negotiations.

To begin, let's dive into one of the most powerful tools at your disposal: the internet. This vast network provides access to platforms where you can research industry standards and salary benchmarks. Websites like Payscale, Glassdoor, and LinkedIn Salary Insights offer detailed breakdowns of salaries across various roles and industries. These resources allow you to compare your current or prospective salary to others in similar positions, giving you a solid foundation for establishing your worth. Not only can these platforms shed light on base pay, but they also often provide insights into total compensation packages, including bonuses, stock options, and other benefits.

Beyond salary data, industry-specific forums and professional networks are treasure troves of additional information. Engaging with online communities such as Reddit, Quora, or niche professional groups on LinkedIn, can reveal inside perspectives and advice from those who have walked the path before you. Discussions within these spaces often cover the nuances of negotiation tactics used by different companies, and it's worth participating or observing to gain insights you might not find elsewhere.

Another key tool lies in leveraging professional associations and trade groups. These organizations often have up-to-date reports and whitepapers reflecting current market conditions and trends. They can also connect you with seasoned professionals and mentors who might provide firsthand advice or even role-playing opportunities to practice your negotiation skills.

But it's not just online resources that can prepare you. Local libraries and community centers frequently offer workshops and seminars on career development topics, including negotiation. Though they may seem like traditional resources, they can provide valuable networking opportunities and access to advice from experts in the field.

Technology also lends a creative edge to research and preparation through digital applications designed to optimize productivity and focus. Apps like Evernote, Notion, and Trello can help you organize your thoughts, store notes, and track your progress as you prepare for negotiation. These tools allow you to sort and prioritize your research, ensuring that you arrive at your negotiation armed not only with facts but also with a strategic plan.

For those negotiating in international or cross-cultural contexts, technology offers even more specialized tools. Language translation apps like Google Translate can bridge any potential language gaps, while cultural databases like Hofstede's Insights provide detailed analyses on cultural norms and styles, helping you tailor your approach to suit the global nature of business today.

Let's not forget the role of virtual meeting platforms and communication tools in negotiation. Familiarizing yourself with platforms such as Zoom, Microsoft Teams, or Slack can ease the technical burden of remote negotiations, allowing you to focus on delivering your message effectively. Features such as screen sharing can be used to present data or proposals visually, making your case more compelling.

Looming large are tools that provide feedback and training in communication skills. Technologies such as AI-based coaching apps offer simulations in negotiation scenarios, offering a safe space to practice and receive constructive critiques. This technology can help refine your tone, pacing, and word choice, maximizing clarity and impact during actual negotiation discussions.

Additionally, apps focused on emotional intelligence, like How We Feel, can guide you in managing stress and anxiety which often accompany high-stakes negotiations. These tools help you develop resilience and maintain composure, ensuring that you're negotiating from a position of strength rather than tension.

While tools and resources are incredibly helpful, the magic happens when you synthesize this information to create a powerful narrative articulating your value. This involves weaving your research and insights into a compelling story that aligns your market worth with your desired outcomes. Remember, technology is a conduit, a medium through which your preparation translates into tangible negotiation success.

In summary, effectively using technology to your advantage in salary negotiation begins with comprehensive research and thoughtful preparation. The tools you choose to employ can transform vague aspirations into actionable strategies, setting you on the path toward achieving the salary and benefits you rightfully deserve. As you embrace these resources, know that you're refining not only your strategy but also building confidence and honing skills that will serve you across the breadth of your career.

Enhancing Communication with Technology

In our hyper-connected world, technology is a powerful ally in salary negotiation. It's not just a tool but a bridge that empowers clear, effective dialogue. Whether you're a seasoned professional or just entering the workforce, leveraging technology for communication can significantly influence your negotiation outcomes.

First and foremost, digital tools like email and instant messaging platforms have transformed how we communicate in the workplace. They provide a written record of discussions, which is crucial during negotiations. This means you can easily refer back to previous conversations and ensure nothing is left misunderstood. More importantly, a well-crafted email can serve as a strategic follow-up to verbal negotiations, reiterating key points and keeping discussions on track. It serves as a formal reminder of commitments made by both parties, minimizing the risk of miscommunication.

Video conferencing tools such as Zoom, Microsoft Teams, and Google Meet have become integral, especially with the rise of remote work. The ability to engage face-to-face, even virtually, adds a valuable layer of personal interaction that goes beyond written text. Visual cues and tone of voice can add depth to your negotiation style, presenting you as confident and personable. The key is practicing effective verbal communication, ensuring your points are delivered with clarity and confidence even when miles apart.

To maximize these interactions, prepare your digital environment as if it were a physical meeting room. Professionalism should extend to how your space appears onscreen. An uncluttered, well-lit background, good sound quality, and dressing appropriately go a long way in making a strong impression. These small details underscore your seriousness in negotiation and can subtly influence a potential raise or offer. Remember, consistency in professionalism across all forms of communication reinforces your reliability and value.

Technology also offers incredible resources for crafting your negotiation strategy. Tools like LinkedIn, Glassdoor, and Payscale provide insights into industry standards, salary benchmarks, and company cultures. By gathering data, you're equipped with facts rather than assumptions, making your salary requests more compelling. The ability to provide tangible evidence during discussions can tip the scales in your favor.

Moreover, there are various apps and digital platforms specifically designed to refine communication skills. Applications offering negotiation simulations and skill-building exercises help in honing your approach, providing a safe space to practice and adjust tactics. Feedback from these platforms guides improvements in real-world negotiations, reducing anxiety when it's time to engage in actual discussions.

Social media can serve as a professional networking tool, essential for negotiating in today's market. Platforms like Twitter, LinkedIn, and even professional forums allow you to connect with industry leaders and peers, who can provide insights and advice or even support your negotiation efforts. Engaging in discussions, sharing industry-related content, and staying active in your community positions you as an informed and involved professional.

One major advantage of using technology is the potential to leverage artificial intelligence (AI) and machine learning. There are smart tools that analyze conversations, suggesting improvements or offering alternative phrasing to achieve desired outcomes. AI-driven insights can help identify areas where communication may falter, enabling you to proactively address them. These technologies can also assist in the emotional and behavioral analysis of negotiation partners, offering a deeper understanding of what might persuade them the most effectively.

Despite its benefits, technology is not infallible. Over-reliance on digital communication can sometimes strip away the nuances that come with face-to-face interactions. Therefore, it's crucial to balance tech use with traditional interpersonal skills. Focus on active listening, maintaining eye contact during video calls, and being mindful of your speech pace and tone. These human elements are irreplaceable and undeniably powerful when combined with digital tools.

In summary, technology isn't a substitute for great communication skills but a complement. By integrating digital tools thoughtfully, you can navigate salary negotiations with an enhanced sense of control and precision. From gathering intel to refining your delivery, technology provides multifaceted support that can elevate your negotiation game significantly. Embrace the opportunities these tools offer, and you'll find yourself more prepared, more confident, and ultimately more successful in securing the compensation you deserve.

Chapter 16:
Negotiating Benefits and Perks

When it comes to salary negotiations, many focus primarily on the dollar figure, yet understanding and negotiating benefits and perks can significantly enhance your overall compensation package and job satisfaction. Often, these non-salary components offer value that surpasses mere financial remuneration. Before stepping into negotiations, have a clear understanding of what's important to you — whether it's flexible working hours, additional vacation days, health benefits, or professional development opportunities. By conducting thorough research on industry standards and your personal priorities, you harness the ability to craft persuasive arguments tailored to both your needs and the employer's capabilities. Strategically addressing benefits also demonstrates your comprehensive understanding of organizational value structures, enhancing your positioning as a thoughtful and resourceful candidate. Keep in mind, negotiating these perks is not just an addendum to salary talks but a crucial component that reflects your holistic view of career satisfaction. As you engage in these discussions, remain open and creative, ensuring that the final agreement not only meets but potentially exceeds your expectations.

Understanding the Value of Non-Salary Benefits

It's easy to focus solely on the numbers when entering a salary negotiation. After all, the paycheck is a tangible and immediate reflection of our value at work. However, looking at compensation through a broader lens reveals the wealth of benefits extending beyond just the salary. These non-salary benefits can greatly enhance your overall financial and personal well-being, offering both immediate and long-term advantages.

Non-salary benefits are a crucial part of the complete compensation package and can sometimes even compensate for a lower salary. These benefits may include health insurance, retirement contributions, paid time off, flexible work arrangements, and professional development opportunities, among others. Understanding and effectively negotiating these benefits can significantly bolster your career satisfaction and financial security.

One of the primary reasons non-salary benefits are so valuable is they often provide a level of financial security beyond what a paycheck can. Consider health insurance: it's a critical benefit that can save you thousands of dollars annually. In cases where the employer covers most, if not all, of the premium costs, this benefit becomes a financial cushion. Similarly, retirement plans like 401(k) contributions offered by employers can have lasting impacts by compounding over the years, ensuring a comfortable lifestyle post-retirement.

But the value of non-salary benefits isn't exclusively monetary. Benefits like flexible working hours or the ability to work remotely can greatly enhance your work-life balance. These offerings allow for better time management, reducing stress and potentially increasing productivity. When you're able to mold your work environment to suit your personal life, job satisfaction tends to soar.

Let's not overlook paid time off (PTO). When effectively negotiated, PTO can ensure that employees have the necessary time to recharge, contribute to their well-being, and avoid burnout. This period allows professionals to step back, gain perspective, and come back ready to perform at their peak. Access to generous PTO policies often becomes a deciding factor for many when evaluating job offers.

Professional development and learning opportunities provided by employers are another form of enriching benefits. They offer the chance to expand your skill set, stay updated with industry advancements, and increase your marketability. Employers that invest in your growth signal that they value your career development and see it as mutually beneficial. Attending workshops, obtaining certifications, or furthering education, supported by employer sponsorship, could be your stepping stone to higher earning potential in the future.

Understanding the value of non-salary benefits also involves recognizing the impact they have on family and personal aspects of life. Family-oriented benefits like parental leave and childcare assistance can be game changers. For many professionals, these benefits greatly enhance their capacity to balance work demands with family responsibilities effectively. Happy employees often lead to higher retention rates, which reflects back positively on workplace morale and productivity.

Negotiating these benefits requires as much, if not more, preparation than salary discussions. It's vital to assess which benefits hold the greatest value to you personally. If you're health-conscious, a comprehensive insurance plan might be your priority. If you're aiming for long-term career growth, educational reimbursements might top your list. By knowing what matters most to you, you align your negotiation strategies with your life and career goals.

Discussing non-salary benefits effectively in negotiations necessitates a shift in approach. While salary figures might revolve around market rates and economic conditions, non-salary benefits afford more flexibility. Most companies have varied policies regarding benefits, and expressing a genuine interest in these can often lead to a more collaborative negotiation atmosphere. When broaching the topic, express how specific benefits will enhance your ability to contribute positively to the organization.

While you've got the spotlight, articulate to the employer why these benefits are important to you and how they align with your career goals and personal needs. Use this opportunity to display a mutual understanding of the company's culture and values. Engage in a dialogue to explore potential compromises or customizations; often, employers are more adaptable in this domain than with base salary adjustments.

Given that non-salary benefits can also significantly impact tax considerations, it's critical to factor in these practical elements. Some benefits, like company-provided vehicles or travel allowances, come with tax implications. Weigh these potential costs against their advantages to ensure you're making informed decisions.

Remember, emphasizing non-salary benefits isn't just about extracting more from the employer. It's about constructing a work-life framework that accentuates your professional growth and personal contentment. When integrated effectively into your compensation package, these benefits can contribute immensely to your career journey, elevating both your professional and personal facets of life.

Ultimately, understanding the value of non-salary benefits transforms the negotiation process into a collaboration rather than a competition. It opens doors to discussions that are as much about mutual alignment as they are about personal advantage. As you navigate these conversations, keep in mind that you're not merely negotiating terms; you're shaping the landscape of your professional experience.

Strategies for Benefits Negotiation

When it comes to negotiating benefits, many people underestimate their importance in the overall compensation package. However, benefits and perks can sometimes make a substantial difference in job satisfaction and financial security. Understanding how to negotiate these elements skillfully can provide you with a competitive edge and enhance your work-life balance significantly.

To start, it's crucial to have a clear picture of what's important to you. Before entering negotiations, make a list of benefits and perks that align with your personal and professional goals. This could include health insurance, retirement contributions, flexible work hours, or even professional development opportunities. Knowing what you want provides direction and helps you prioritize during discussions.

One powerful strategy is to gather information about industry standards for benefits. Much like salary research, understanding what competitors offer can serve as a benchmark. This information will enable you to identify any gaps in your current offer and justify your requests with evidence of industry norms. Remember, data equips you to negotiate from a position of knowledge rather than guesswork.

Building on the principle of understanding your value, frame your requests in terms of mutual benefits. Explain how certain benefits could enhance your productivity or job satisfaction, which in turn benefits the employer. For instance, if you're asking for flexible work arrangements, make a case for how this can lead to improved efficiency and reduced burnout.

Timing is also an essential factor in successful benefits negotiation. Consider discussing benefits once salary negotiations are nearing completion or if it becomes apparent that your salary request may not be fully met. This can act as a compromise and demonstrate flexibility on your part while still securing valuable additions to your compensation package. Timing benefits requests strategically ensures that discussions do not derail or diminish the perceived value of your salary.

Employ a collaborative negotiation approach rather than a confrontational one. By involving the employer in the discussion about benefits and seeking to understand their constraints and priorities, you show a willingness to work together towards a satisfactory outcome. This collaborative stance can build rapport and increase the likelihood that you will leave the negotiation table with a favorable package.

Furthermore, advocating for yourself with confidence and clarity is vital. Clearly articulate why certain benefits are important to you and how they affect your decision-making. Personalize the conversation by sharing relevant anecdotes or reasoning that highlights these benefits' significance in your life or career. Be assertive, yet respectful, ensuring the tone remains professional and constructive.

Don't be afraid to think creatively about benefits. Employers may have limitations on traditional benefits but could be open to more innovative solutions. Consider proposing unique perks that could benefit you and be a viable option for the employer, such as additional paid time off, wellness stipends, or remote work opportunities.

Furthermore, understanding the employer's perspective is fundamental. If an employer is hesitant to expand on particular benefits, inquire about their reasoning. This opens a pathway for dialogue and can lead to tailored solutions that fit both parties' needs. Being aware of the constraints and working within them shows adaptability and increases your chance of securing adjustments where possible.

When concluding discussions, ensure commitments regarding benefits are documented. It's vital to have all agreed-upon terms included in your employment agreement or offer letter. This eliminates ambiguities and ensures that promises made during negotiations are honored throughout your tenure with the company.

In summary, negotiating benefits requires a multifaceted approach. It involves researching industry standards, prioritizing personal needs, timing requests strategically, and engaging in collaborative dialogue. With these strategies, you bolster your negotiating skillset beyond salary discussions alone, enhancing your overall compensation and aligning your work situation with personal and professional aspirations.

Chapter 17:
Long-Term Salary Growth

When it comes to long-term salary growth, it's not just about the immediate gains but setting yourself up for sustained success. Think of it as planting seeds today for the harvest of tomorrow. Start by envisioning your professional journey, identifying key milestones that align with your career goals, and strategically planning salary reviews around these advancements. The foundation of this growth lies in consistently proving your value and aligning your contributions with the company's objectives. By maintaining open lines of communication with employers, you can understand and influence how your role can expand in alignment with broader business goals. Remember, regular skills enhancement, networking, and staying informed about industry trends empower you to command a higher salary over time. Turn your career into a story of continuous growth by mastering the art of leveraging your achievements and negotiating strategic raises that don't just reflect your past performance but anticipate your future potential.

Planning for Future Increases

In the realm of salary negotiation, obtaining a pay increase isn't merely an endpoint—it's part of a broader strategy for long-term career growth. Planning for future increases requires foresight, diligence, and a proactive mindset. This section will explore how you can cultivate a vision for your financial trajectory and maintain upward momentum in your earnings.

One of the most essential steps in planning for future salary increases is to clearly define your long-term career goals. Consider where you want to be five, ten, or even twenty years from now. Do you see yourself in a leadership position? Are you aiming to branch out into a different industry or establish your own business? By having a firm grasp on your professional ambitions, you can chart a path that aligns your financial growth with your career objectives.

After setting your long-term goals, break them down into achievable milestones. If your goal is to double your salary within a decade, determine what incremental increases you'll need along the way. This approach not only makes your ultimate goal more attainable but also provides benchmarks against which you can measure your progress.

Regularly reassessing your market value is another critical practice. The job market is dynamic, with industries experiencing shifts that can influence salary trends. Stay informed of salary ranges for your position, sector, and geographic location by consulting resources like industry reports, salary surveys, and professional networks. By maintaining an updated understanding of your worth, you can ensure that your compensation keeps pace with market standards.

Education and skill development are vital components of planning for salary growth. Today's competitive job arena demands continual learning. Identifying key skills that are in demand—be they technical proficiencies, leadership capabilities, or specialized knowledge—can elevate your value to current and prospective employers. Consider pursuing certifications, attending workshops, or enrolling in advanced degree programs that align with industry needs.

Building strong relationships within your professional network can also support your salary growth. Networking offers insights into emerging opportunities and innovative practices. By establishing connections with industry leaders and peers, you can leverage their guidance and resources to enhance your career strategy. Mentorship can be particularly beneficial, providing you with personalized advice from those who have successfully navigated similar paths.

Successful negotiation for salary increases often involves timing and strategy. Recognizing when to initiate a salary discussion is crucial. Align your requests with your organization's financial schedules, such as budget planning cycles or annual reviews. Additionally, choose moments when your value is most apparent—perhaps after achieving a significant accomplishment or when you've taken on new responsibilities.

In preparing your case for a salary increase, articulate your accomplishments and contributions clearly. Highlight how your efforts have positively impacted the organization's objectives or bottom line. Quantifying your achievements—such as revenue growth, cost savings, or increased efficiency—provides tangible evidence of your worth and builds a compelling case for a raise.

Future salary growth is a partnership between you and your employer. Open, honest communication about your career aspirations and the value you bring can create a cooperative environment conducive to salary increases. Regularly scheduled performance reviews are opportunities to discuss your development trajectory and set expectations for future compensation adjustments.

Furthermore, being receptive to feedback and demonstrating a willingness to improve can enhance your prospects for raises. Employers value team members who are committed to growth and development. By acting on constructive criticism and continuously seeking ways to enhance your performance, you reinforce your dedication and potential for greater contributions.

Finally, embrace a mindset of resilience and adaptability. Economic fluctuations, organizational changes, or industry disruptions can challenge even the best-laid plans. However, by remaining flexible and responsive to these changes, you can identify new opportunities for growth and navigate shifts in the job landscape more effectively.

Planning for future salary increases isn't simply about securing more money—it's about building the foundation for a sustainable and fulfilling career. With defined goals, strategic planning, and an ongoing commitment to your personal and professional development, you can confidently navigate your journey toward greater financial success.

Building a Career with Strategic Raises

In the journey toward long-term salary growth, securing strategic raises is a crucial component. It's not just about asking for a bump in pay; it's about architecting a pathway that aligns with both your career aspirations and the value you bring to your organization. To build a career on strategic raises, you need more than just guts and timing—you need a comprehensive understanding of how to present your achievements and future potential in a way that resonates with decision-makers.

Strategic raises start with the groundwork. Before entering any negotiation, lay a solid foundation by documenting your accomplishments, quantifying your contributions, and understanding the market standards for your role. This preparation helps you articulate your value, which is pivotal when discussing raises. But the documentation isn't just about creating a list; it's about telling a story that links your growth and contributions to organizational success.

One effective strategy is to align personal development goals with the company's objectives. By syncing your ambitions with the organization's vision, you emphasize not only your dedication but also your potential to contribute significantly. Express clear, measurable goals during performance reviews that illustrate how your growth could enhance company performance. This clarity turns your raise request into a mutual growth proposition rather than a mere plea for more cash.

Timing is everything in negotiations, especially when it comes to raises. Understanding the financial health of your company, as well as scheduling your discussions at the right time (such as during budget planning phases), can significantly impact your chances of success. It's not only about when to ask but also what context surrounds your request—like recent successful project completions or receiving notable client accolades.

The role of communication in building a career with strategic raises cannot be overstated. Be articulate and precise about your accomplishments and future contributions. Confidence does not mean arrogance. While it's vital to advocate for yourself, ensure your communication style remains collaborative. Use active listening to understand your employer's perspective and address any concerns they might have regarding resource allocation.

Overcoming employers' potential reservations about raises involves using psychological principles effectively. Employ empathy to forecast their objections and prepare counterpoints. Utilize the anchoring effect by starting with a salary figure that comfortably exceeds your lowest acceptable offer. Through these tactics, you establish a norm from which negotiations can proceed favorably.

Networking goes hand in hand with achieving strategic raises. Building a rapport with mentors and allies in your industry can provide insights and leverage unseen opportunities. Constantly enhancing your skills not only increases your marketability but keeps you ahead of industry trends, which can open doors to unexpected raises as you become a crucial asset to your company.

There's also a significant importance in setting a timeline for your career growth and aligning your raise requests with these checkpoints. Setting these milestones reflects seriousness in your career planning, enabling you to map out a long-term strategy that involves incremental raises and potentially even changes in role or responsibility.

Finally, persistence and adaptability are key attributes for achieving strategic raises. If you're initially turned down, use that as an opportunity to understand what can be done differently next time. Seek feedback and adjust your performance and proposals accordingly. Turning rejections into constructive feedback loops allows you to refine your approach for future success.

In summary, building a career with strategic raises is about more than just money. It's about aligning your career path with strategic contributions to your organization. By documenting achievements, syncing personal and professional goals, timing your negotiations, employing effective communication strategies, leveraging your network, and learning from rejections, you not only improve your chances for raises but craft a career trajectory that leads to sustained growth and satisfaction.

Chapter 18:
Legal and Ethical Considerations

As you develop more nuanced salary negotiation skills, it's crucial to have a solid understanding of the legal and ethical landscape you're maneuvering through. Knowledge of employment contract clauses can arm you with foresight, allowing you to set clear expectations and shield yourself from potential pitfalls. These legal frameworks, while protective, also compel us to adhere to ethical negotiation practices. Integrity is not just moral—it fosters trust and lasting professional relationships. When you negotiate transparently and fairly, you're not merely advocating for better compensation; you're also ensuring that the professional space remains respectful and equitable. Embrace these considerations as part of your negotiation toolkit, as they serve as the guardrails that guide and support your career journey while maintaining a strong ethical foundation.

Understanding Employment Contract Clauses

You're sitting across from a potential employer, and everything seems promising. They've discussed job responsibilities, salary, and all those enticing perks. Yet, before smiling and accepting the offer, it's vital to pause and delve into a critical aspect often overlooked in the excitement: the employment contract. While negotiating your salary can set the stage for financial success, understanding the nuances of an employment contract can secure your professional future in less obvious ways.

Employment contracts aren't just formalities; they're the backbone of your professional agreement. They define your role's scope, set expectations, and outline the legal parameters of your employment. A well-crafted contract can protect both you and your employer, reducing misunderstandings and providing a clear framework for your working relationship. Conversely, a poorly written or misunderstood contract could bind you to unfavorable terms.

Let's begin with the basic structure often found in employment contracts. Most contracts will include provisions regarding job role and responsibilities, start date, compensation package including salary and benefits, working hours, and termination clauses. While some of these may appear straightforward, the devil is in the details.

Firstly, examine the clauses related to job responsibilities. Ensure that these align with what was discussed during interviews. Ambiguities here could lead to role creep, where additional duties gradually become part of your routine without any corresponding increase in compensation. This is where clarity can serve as your ally. Ask questions about any vague wording to ensure both parties share the same understanding of your role.

The compensation section may initially seem the simplest: it's about your pay, after all. However, beyond the base salary, the contract should detail bonus structures, commissions if applicable, and any increment criteria. Will your performance be reviewed annually, and what are the key performance indicators? These details pave the path to future raises and bonuses. Notably, lack of specifics can leave significant room for interpretation, often to the employer's advantage.

Consideration of termination clauses is crucial. These clauses determine the conditions under which you or your employer can end the employment relationship. Some contracts include probationary periods during which termination may require less notice. Equally significant is whether severance is stipulated. Should you decide to leave, knowing your exit terms will help avoid legal hurdles.

In a world where remote work is becoming more normalized, pay attention to any clauses that discuss remote work or telecommuting policies. These may define expectations for work-from-home arrangements, such as required meeting attendance or office check-ins, and might even include stipulations about changing these arrangements.

Non-compete and non-disclosure agreements are common in many industries and can have far-reaching implications for your career. A non-compete clause might restrict you from working with competitors post-employment, so scrutinize its geographical and time limitations to ensure they're reasonable. Non-disclosure agreements, meanwhile, aim to protect proprietary information, but they shouldn't unreasonably limit your future employment opportunities.

Intellectual property clauses are often tucked within contracts, specifying that any inventions or creations during your tenure belong to the company. While standard in many fields, these clauses can be negotiated, particularly if you're in a creative or technical role where individual innovation is likely. Make sure your own creations outside of work aren't unintentionally claimed.

Moreover, ensure there are clauses that address work-life balance, such as paid time off, family leave, and health benefits. With rising awareness about mental health, more contracts are incorporating wellness programs. It's essential that these benefits are clearly articulated so you can hold your employer accountable should discrepancies arise.

Ultimately, understanding employment contract clauses boils down to a mix of due diligence and communication. Approach the contract review as a negotiation in itself. If terms are unclear or unsatisfactory, don't hesitate to raise them. Employers expect questions and often appreciate the thoroughness it demonstrates. Your willingness to discuss shows your commitment to a fair, transparent working relationship.

Contracts are legally binding, so before signing, consider seeking legal or professional advice, especially for high-stakes positions. Attorneys experienced in employment law can provide essential insight into whether the terms are standard or require negotiation.

Your employment contract is a safeguard—a written assurance of your role, benefits, and employment guidelines. Approaching contracts with a strategic mindset can solidify your professional standing and aid in confidently navigating your career. Knowledge is power, and understanding your contract not only supports your current job but can influence your professional journey well into the future.

Mastering employment contract clauses goes hand in hand with enhancing your salary negotiation skills. As we journey through this book, you'll continue to gather tools and insights that will equip you to walk into any negotiation or contract review feeling prepared and self-assured.

Ethical Negotiation Practices

Negotiation is an art that, when practiced ethically, reflects not only skill but also integrity and mutual respect. In the realm of salary discussions, ethical negotiation practices go beyond securing a favorable outcome; they ensure that the process honors all parties involved. These practices instill a sense of trust and fairness, crucial elements that often determine the long-term success of any professional relationship. Embodying ethical standards means negotiating without resorting to deceit or manipulation, opting instead for transparency and honesty.

An ethical approach in negotiations begins with respect for the other party. Understanding your employer's perspective doesn't signify agreement with everything they propose but demonstrates an appreciation for their position. An ethical negotiator listens attentively, acknowledging the employer's constraints and goals. This mutual understanding fosters a collaborative environment, looking to resolve differences amicably rather than turning the process into a battleground.

Transparency in communication is another cornerstone of ethical negotiation. Being upfront about your expectations, needs, and limitations sets a positive tone. It opens a dialogue where both sides can express their needs without fear of being blindsided. Ethical practices discourage withholding crucial information to gain an edge and instead advocate for a clear and honest exchange. Transparency doesn't mean divulging every detail but rather paints an accurate picture of what you bring to the table and what you seek in return.

Another important ethical consideration is maintaining honesty throughout the negotiation process. Honesty builds trust, and trust facilitates a smoother negotiation. When you present your case, whether it's about your market value or the specialized knowledge you bring, it's essential to rely on factual and accurate information. Exaggerating skills or misrepresenting previous positions can lead to a breached trust, damaging not only the negotiation outcome but also your professional reputation.

Confidentiality also plays a vital role in ethical negotiations. Information shared during these discussions often includes sensitive company details and personal data, all of which should be handled with utmost discretion. Demonstrating respect for confidentiality reassures the employer of your professionalism, a trait that extends beyond the negotiation table and into your working tenure. Avoiding the disclosure of shared information highlights a commitment to ethical standards and reflects your dependability as an employee.

Patience and empathy serve as guiding virtues in ethical negotiations. The ability to empathize with an employer's position and exercise patience can transform tense discussions into productive conversations. Ethical negotiators recognize the importance of timing and are patient enough to understand that successful negotiations may require multiple rounds of discussions. This patience allows for thorough understanding and consideration of all variables, leading to decisions that benefit all parties involved.

Furthermore, ethical negotiation practices involve creating win-win scenarios. Rather than viewing negotiations as zero-sum games where one party's gain is another's loss, seek solutions that deliver value to everyone. This mindset not only aids in obtaining better salary packages but also nurtures positive long-term professional relationships. Ethical negotiators ask questions like, "How can we maximize benefits on both sides?" or "What solutions address both my needs and the company's objectives?" This approach fosters creative problem-solving and reinforces ethical principles.

Ethical negotiation extends beyond the immediate conversation and includes following up on commitments made during negotiations. Whether it's an agreement on salary adjustments, work responsibilities, or future opportunities for growth, ethical practices demand accountability. Following through on promises establishes a foundation of reliability and demonstrates a consistent dedication to ethical standards, reinforcing the trust built during negotiations.

In addition, ethical negotiators maintain humility and grace throughout the process. They acknowledge the challenges both parties face and exhibit gratitude, regardless of the negotiation's outcome. This attitude not only enriches the immediate negotiation but also enhances future interactions, reflecting positively on your professional demeanor.

A critical part of ethical negotiation is also knowing when to walk away. If terms become untenable or compromise core values, ethical negotiators recognize the importance of maintaining personal integrity over immediate gains. Walking away is not a sign of failure but rather a principled decision prioritizing long-term ethical standards over short-term benefits.

Legal considerations play a role in ethical negotiation as well. Understanding employment laws and company policies ensures that your negotiation practices remain within the legal framework. This knowledge not only safeguards you from potential legal pitfalls but strengthens your position as an informed negotiator who respects and adheres to legal and ethical obligations.

Ethical negotiation isn't an innate skill but rather a discipline cultivated over time. It's about consciously choosing respect, fairness, and integrity in every interaction. The resultant trust and respect are invaluable, far surpassing any immediate financial gain derived through unscrupulous means. With each negotiation, you refine the art, ensuring that you not only benefit personally but also contribute positively to the professional community at large.

Ultimately, ethical negotiation practices enhance not only your salary negotiation skills but also strengthen your character. In an ever-evolving professional landscape, these practices act as a compass, steering you toward decisions that sustain growth, mutual respect, and enduring professional relationships. As you navigate your negotiation journey, let ethics guide you, ensuring that each step taken is marked by integrity and respect.

Chapter 19:
Negotiating for New Positions

Stepping into a new job opportunity can be as thrilling as it is daunting, but understanding how to negotiate your position is key to securing a rewarding start. As you venture into this new chapter, consider the full spectrum of the job offer—from salary to responsibilities and even location flexibility. Start by meticulously researching your prospective employer and industry standards, equipping yourself with a data-backed understanding of your market worth. As you engage in discussions, articulate your value proposition clearly, emphasizing the unique skills and experiences you bring to the table. Keep your long-term career path in mind and aim to structure agreements that allow for future growth and adaptability. This approach not only affirms your readiness but also builds a foundation of respect and collaboration with your new employer. Remember, the goal is to align the offer with your career aspirations while ensuring the transition into your new role is as seamless and empowering as possible.

Strategies for Job Offer Negotiations

Landing a new job is an exciting milestone, yet it also marks the beginning of a critical phase: negotiating your job offer. This is not merely about discussing numbers and figures; it's an intricate dance involving mental preparation, strategic communication, and an understanding of psychology. No matter your field or level of experience, developing strategies to negotiate job offers is essential to securing a position under terms that reflect your worth.

At the heart of a successful negotiation lies thorough preparation. Start by grounding yourself in knowledge. Research the market to understand salary standards for your role, industry, and geographic location. Websites like Glassdoor and Payscale can provide valuable insights, giving you confidence in your position. Knowing your worth allows you to anchor the conversation effectively, setting a baseline that ensures you're not underselling yourself from the get-go.

But knowing the market is just one part of the equation. It's equally important to reflect on your unique contributions. Ask yourself, "What specific skills and experiences do I bring to this role?" Articulate your value in terms of previous successes, specialized skills, and potential impact on the new organization. A pitch that highlights your contributions can transform the negotiation into a discussion about mutual benefit rather than a simple transaction of services for salary.

Timing is another crucial element. Approach negotiations with patience and tact. The initial offer might come during the interview process or after you've received a formal job offer. Yet, regardless of when it's presented, recognizing the delicate balance between eagerness and prudence is key. An immediate counteroffer might give the impression of rashness, while a delayed response could suggest disinterest. Navigating this timeline thoughtfully can keep negotiations amicable and professional.

Communication is the bridge that turns preparation into successful negotiation. Clear, concise, and assertive dialogue helps convey your expectations without hostility or arrogance. Use "I" statements to express your needs, such as "I would feel comfortable with a salary in the range of..." This approach affirms your perspective while maintaining the collaborative spirit of the negotiation.

Leveraging psychological principles can also give you an edge. Anchoring, for example, is a potent psychological effect where the first number thrown into a discussion tends to heavily influence the final outcome. If possible, aim to set the initial range yourself with figures slightly above your minimum requirement. This establishes a high anchor point that can steer subsequent discussions towards your target.

Active listening is another powerful tool. Paying close attention to the employer's responses can reveal hidden opportunities and constraints, allowing you to adapt your strategy. For instance, if a company expresses budgetary limits, explore other avenues of compensation such as bonuses, stock options, or additional vacation days. These benefits, although not immediately evident in a paycheck, significantly enhance your overall package.

That said, never underestimate the importance of flexibility. Successful negotiations often involve compromise. While it's essential to stand your ground on critical points, showing willingness to find middle ground on others can foster goodwill and result in a more satisfactory outcome for both parties. This balance between firmness and adaptability can shape the tone of your future working relationship, building trust and respect right from the start.

Furthermore, confidence is key. It's natural to feel apprehensive, especially if you're new to negotiating. However, remember that a job offer negotiation is a standard part of the hiring process. Employers often expect and respect candidates who negotiate, recognizing it as a sign of professionalism and self-worth. Approaching the negotiation confidently can alter the dynamics in your favor, presenting you as a competent individual who understands their value.

Yet, confidence doesn't mean you should inflate your demands beyond reason. Instead, use it to assertively present well-researched arguments for your proposals. You're not just asking for more money;

you're articulating a more comprehensive story about your potential contributions to the company. This narrative should be supported by facts, such as metrics from past projects or clear examples of how you've driven value in previous roles.

Ultimately, preparation, communication, psychological insight, and confidence weave together to create a robust strategy for job offer negotiations. As you refine these skills, remember that each negotiation is an opportunity for learning. Whether the outcome aligns perfectly with your expectations or not, the experience sharpens your negotiation acumen, preparing you for future opportunities.

Your journey in negotiation extends beyond this single moment. It's a lifelong skill that will benefit you in salary discussions, job transitions, and even daily work interactions. By approaching it strategically, you not only aim for financial gain but also set the stage for a career that aligns closely with your goals and aspirations. As you practice and grow, you'll find yourself not only negotiating for a job but shaping your professional journey with purpose and poise.

Embrace each negotiation as a key chapter in your career story, one where you're the author, crafting narratives of success powered by the strength and wisdom of strategic negotiation. Remember, the most effective negotiations are not a win-lose scenario but a collaborative effort towards a mutually beneficial agreement where both sides walk away feeling valued and satisfied.

Transitioning into a New Role with Confidence

Stepping into a new role is a transformative experience, filled with both excitement and apprehension. As you've effectively navigated the negotiation process and secured a new position, the next phase is all about carrying that momentum forward. Confidence is key in this transition, shaping not only how others perceive you but also how you perceive yourself. It's a powerful ally in making a strong first impression, establishing your professional presence, and building the trust necessary to succeed in your new role.

The first few weeks in a new position can be overwhelming, as they often bring a barrage of new information, processes, and dynamics. However, embracing a confident mindset can transform these challenges into opportunities. Start by focusing on what you've already achieved—landing the role was a testament to your skills and potential. Remember why you were hired in the first place. This role aligns with your capabilities, and you have the competence to excel in it.

Establishing confidence begins with preparation. Knowledge truly is power. Spend time understanding the company's culture, its goals, and the expectations for your role. Immerse yourself in any available resources, documents, or communications you can find. The more informed you are, the more assured you'll feel. Preparation diminishes uncertainty and empowers you to participate in discussions and decisions effectively.

Another tool in building confidence during this transition is leveraging your previous successes. Take stock of past achievements and reflect on how those experiences have equipped you with unique insights and perspectives. These reflections serve as firm reminders of your capabilities, providing a reassuring internal narrative. Use these accomplishments as a foundation to build upon and as a reminder of the value you bring to your new role.

Next, seek out opportunities to engage with your new team and learn about their priorities and challenges. Establishing rapport early on is crucial, not just for building a network of allies but also for understanding the nuances of your team's working style. Whether through formal meetings or informal conversations, genuineness and openness will help you make these connections. Being active in your engagement shows your commitment to integrating into the existing team dynamic.

However, it's essential to manage your expectations. You're not expected to know everything right away. Allow yourself the grace to be a learner. Ask questions, seek feedback, and be open to new ways of doing things. Demonstrating a willingness to learn showcases emotional intelligence and humility—both vital attributes of a confident leader. Over time, as you gather insights and build relationships, your confidence will naturally grow.

Embrace professional development opportunities that come your way. Companies often offer mentorship programs, training, and workshops. These resources can aid your integration process by broadening your skills and understanding of your role. Additionally, expressing interest in professional growth initiatives demonstrates your commitment to self-improvement and your enthusiasm for the position.

As you settle into your new role, set realistic and achievable goals. While ambition is encouraged, overburdening yourself with unachievable targets can erode confidence. Begin by setting short-term objectives that align with larger company goals. Achieving these milestones can provide a sense of accomplishment and boost your confidence gradually. Over time, as you consistently meet these goals, you'll establish a track record of success.

Confidence also involves taking calculated risks. Once you're comfortable with your understanding of the role and the company's operations, look for areas where you can innovate or improve processes. Propose thoughtful ideas and solutions that highlight your expertise and commitment to the company's objectives. Being proactive illustrates your confidence in your capabilities and your desire to contribute meaningfully.

Transition periods are ideal for building resilience—a crucial component of long-term confidence. Learning how to manage setbacks or unexpected challenges gracefully can reinforce your sense of self-belief. View these obstacles as opportunities to learn and adapt. Resilience not only strengthens confidence but also enhances your ability to navigate difficult situations effectively.

Finally, maintaining balance in life contributes significantly to sustaining confidence. A healthy work-life balance ensures you're not only thriving professionally but also taking care of your mental and physical well-being. Adequate rest, exercise, and leisure activities replenish your energy, clarity, and focus, enabling you to perform at your best.

In conclusion, transitioning into a new role with confidence is about leveraging your past, embracing your present, and anticipating your future. Throughout this process, remember to celebrate your victories, no matter how small, and remain patient. Building confidence is an ongoing journey, one that evolves with experience and time in your new role. Armed with preparation, resilience, and a genuine desire to succeed, you're more than equipped to make your new beginning a thriving experience.

Chapter 20:
Negotiating as a Freelancer
or Consultant

As a freelancer or consultant, negotiating effectively isn't just a skill—it's a necessity. Unlike traditional salary negotiation, you're not just advocating for a paycheck; you're defining your value, asserting your expertise, and setting the terms for what could be a pivotal professional relationship. The first step is understanding a potential client's budget while aligning it with your worth. This dance involves balancing flexibility with firmness, ensuring that your rates reflect the quality and benefit you bring without pricing yourself out of opportunities. Establishing clear contracts is crucial, as they not only safeguard your interests but also clarify expectations, reducing friction down the line. Each negotiation is a chance to exercise your psychological acumen and persuasive prowess, positioning yourself not just as a hire, but as a strategic partner in your clients' success. This chapter dives into the nuances of setting rates and crafting contracts that underscore the value you deliver, offering the right tactics to turn prospects into long-term, fruitful engagements.

Dealing with Client Budgets

Negotiating as a freelancer or consultant is a unique ballgame compared to traditional salary discussions. The fluidity of budgets, varied client priorities, and the sheer diversity of project types can make even the most seasoned negotiators pause. "Dealing with Client Budgets," as a core component of this chapter, aims to equip you with strategies to navigate complex financial landscapes with finesse and confidence. Let's dive into the nuances of discussing money matters when freelancing.

First and foremost, understanding the budget constraints and priorities of a client is crucial. Clients often have differing financial capacities, reflecting the core value they place on the project versus other business needs. Sometimes, clients aren't entirely transparent about their budgetary limits initially. Here is where your skills as a perceptive negotiator come into play. A direct but tactful approach can unlock key information that helps shape the rest of the conversation.

Begin with open-ended conversations. Ask clients about their expectations for the project, emphasizing desired outcomes rather than financial figures right off the bat. This technique allows you to gather insights into what they value. From here, you can gently steer the conversation toward their financial constraints. Questions like, "Can you offer more context about the allocation for this project?" can unearth pivotal details about the available budget.

Tailoring your pitch according to the discovered budget can make your proposal more palatable to a client. But it's not just about meeting the client where they are. Such adjustments should always spotlight the intrinsic value you bring to the table. Propose options that align with their financial limitations but also emphasize premium outcomes for an enhanced budget. Having a tiered pricing structure ensures flexibility, offering services at basic, intermediate, and advanced levels.

A common misconception is that agreeing to lower budgets equates to diminishing your worth. This is not true when done strategically. Use these scenarios to negotiate for non-monetary benefits, such as long-term business opportunities or showcasing rights to the completed work. Non-cash perks can sometimes outperform an immediate monetary gain, leading to broader exposure and future freelancing avenues.

Even with all strategies in place, you might encounter rigid budgets that still demand tweaks to your offerings. Knowing the project's scope is essential here. Clearly define deliverables to avoid "scope creep." Each adjustment to your services should be underpinned by clear communication to prevent unexpected workload that does not equate to the agreed compensation.

The art of knowing when to walk away can't be understated. Not every potential client will align with your business goals, values, or price points. Trust your intuition and experience. If a budget is far from feasible and negotiations have hit a stalemate, it might be best to redirect energy to more viable opportunities. Walking away with professionalism can also leave the door open for future projects when budgets might be more flexible.

It's essential to maintain a repertoire of negotiation tactics beyond the financial discussions. Skills like active listening and empathizing can play vital roles. By understanding the client's perspectives and challenges, you can craft solutions that resonate best with their immediate needs and abilities. This kind of attentiveness can make you an invaluable partner rather than just a vendor.

With the rise of remote work, freelancers often have the globe as their oyster. This has introduced a further layer of complexity to client budget negotiations. Regional financial norms, currency fluctuations, and varying labor laws can all impact how clients perceive and manage their budgets. As a freelancer or consultant, familiarizing yourself with these global considerations is key.

Finally, don't forget the continuous improvement aspect. Learn from each client interaction. Document the outcomes, techniques used, and client responses to refine your skills over time. This ongoing development can better prepare you for future negotiations, potentially turning difficult talks into successful partnerships.

Dealing with client budgets might seem like a tightrope walk between asserting your value and accommodating financial realities. However, with clearly defined strategies, an adaptable mindset, and confidence in articulating your worth, navigating these conversations becomes more manageable and fulfilling. After all, it's not just about reaching an agreement but paving the way for fruitful, long-term collaborations.

Setting Rates and Contracts

As a freelancer or consultant, setting the right rates and drafting effective contracts are essential components of your business strategy. These elements not only ensure your financial well-being but also protect your professional reputation. To begin with, understanding your market worth is crucial. Research plays a pivotal role in this process. You need to assess industry standards, taking into account your skills, experience, and the value you bring to your clients. Doing so allows you to position yourself competitively, while also ensuring you are not underselling your services.

Your rate not only reflects your expertise but also communicates your confidence in your work. It's important to strike a balance here— set your rates too high, and you might scare off potential clients; set them too low, and you might undermine your own value and sustainability. Many freelancers and consultants employ a tiered pricing strategy to offer flexibility. This can involve charging different rates for different levels of service or offering packages that cater to diverse client needs. Such a strategy can appeal to a broader spectrum of clients while ensuring that higher-tier services reflect their added value.

Time management and scope definition are critical in setting rates. Calculating your rates isn't just about setting an hourly fee; it should reflect the complexity of the project and the time required to execute it effectively. Be upfront in establishing clear terms about deliverables, timelines, and payment schedules. Miscommunication around these can lead to disputes down the line. Remember, scope creep can jeopardize your profitability. It is vital to clearly outline what is included in your services and what would incur additional charges.

Contracts play a fundamental role in your business dealings. They are not mere formalities but crucial tools that clarify expectations and responsibilities for both you and your clients. A well-drafted contract is a safeguard against misunderstandings and legal issues. At the very least, every contract should include the project scope, timelines, payment terms, and clauses for revisions and extra work. This serves as protection for both parties and ensures that there's a clear understanding of the project's parameters.

When drafting contracts, consider including a clause that addresses potential delays, both on your part and the client's. This can protect you against the financial impacts of a delayed project. Additionally, addressing intellectual property rights and confidentiality in your contracts is key, particularly when dealing with sensitive information or proprietary content. Such clauses safeguard your work and your client's interests, fostering trust and professionalism.

A successful contract negotiation often hinges on clarity and mutual benefit. Effective negotiation doesn't necessarily mean getting everything you want; instead, it's about reaching an agreement that meets both your needs and those of your client. Active listening is paramount during this phase—understanding what your client values most can provide leverage and allow for creative solutions that feel like a win-win. For instance, if budget constraints are a concern, you might offer scaled-back versions of your services or focus initially on high-impact areas.

It's also important to think long term. Building a strong relationship with your clients can lead to repeat business and referrals. Therefore, approach negotiations with a mindset of building partnerships rather than executing transactions. Demonstrating flexibility when appropriate can contribute to this relationship building, without undermining your integrity or value. It's about creating a balance between being accommodating and maintaining professional boundaries.

Don't neglect the importance of revising contracts periodically. As your business grows and evolves, so too should the terms and conditions of your contracts. Updating them regularly ensures they remain relevant to your current business model and client expectations. Involving legal experts during the drafting or revision process can provide you with the assurance that your contracts comply with legal standards and adequately protect your interests.

Finally, using invoicing software or payment platforms can streamline the financial aspects of your agreements. These tools help automate billing processes, track overdue payments, and maintain a professional image. Clear payment policies, expressed both verbally and in your contracts, reduce ambiguity and protect your cash flow. It's about creating systems that support your business objectives while simplifying administrative tasks.

To wrap up, setting rates and drafting contracts are the pillars of a successful freelance or consulting business. They require a thoughtful blend of market knowledge, self-awareness, and strategic communication. With these elements firmly in place, you'll not only optimize your earnings but also establish a foundation for professional credibility and sustainable growth.

Chapter 21:
Unique Situations in Negotiation

In the realm of salary negotiations, unique situations often require a refined strategy and heightened awareness. Economic downturns, for example, can create a challenging environment for seeking raises, yet they also offer a chance to prove resilience and adaptability. Successfully managing negotiations in such times involves demonstrating your value as indispensable while understanding the broader financial constraints at play. Additionally, receiving counteroffers when considering a new position can be both invigorating and perplexing; it's crucial to weigh them against your long-term goals and aspirations. Similarly, handling simultaneous offers from different companies requires a delicate balance of expressing genuine interest and leveraging each proposal judiciously. In these unique scenarios, the key lies in maintaining clarity of purpose and an adaptable mindset, ensuring that your negotiation approach is as dynamic as the opportunities themselves.

Managing Negotiations During Economic Downturns

Economic downturns bring unique challenges to salary negotiations, affecting the dynamics between employers and employees. When the economy is struggling, companies tighten budgets, and job security becomes a priority for many. But it's also a time when one's negotiating skills can shine, showcasing the ability to secure value in tough times. Understanding the broader economic context informs your strategy and choice of tactics when you approach negotiations during these periods.

In downturns, employers' perceptions often become more conservative. They may be cautious about expanding payroll, offering raises, or hiring additional staff. This environment calls for negotiations that are grounded in empathy and awareness of the organization's challenges. Yet, it's crucial to remember the negotiation isn't just about immediate financial gain. It's about setting a long-term value proposition that appeals to both parties.

Start by gathering as much information as possible about the company's financial health and industry position. Public companies will often publish quarterly reports, and industry news can provide insights into broader trends. Use this information to frame your negotiation not as a request, but as a strategic conversation about mutual benefits. When you can articulate how your skillset helps the company navigate tough times, you anchor yourself as a valuable asset rather than just another expense.

Adjust expectations but don't undervalue your contribution. While it might be tempting to scale back your demands, do so with an eye toward long-term growth. If a direct salary increase isn't feasible, consider proposing a structured plan for future raises tied to personal or company performance metrics. Employers may be more amenable to incremental increases tied to performance or secured by successful completion of key projects, which can make an agreement more palatable during uncertain economic realities.

Benefits and non-monetary perks are often more malleable than salaries during a recession. Companies might have limited cash flow but could still offer alternative forms of compensation. Discuss possibilities like professional development opportunities, flexible working hours, or enhanced job titles that might set the stage for future advancement. By widening the scope of negotiation beyond salary, you increase your chances of coming away with something valuable.

Be prepared to justify your position with concrete examples of your contributions. Highlight accomplishments that have directly affected the company's bottom line or have prepared it for better performance through turbulent times. Emphasize your problem-solving abilities, resilience, and capacity to innovate—qualities highly valued in economic downturns. Your track record can be your greatest advocate during negotiations.

Listening is particularly critical when negotiating in a downturn. Understand what pressures the company is dealing with and what decisions are driving management strategies. Effective listening can uncover mutual interests that weren't immediately apparent and can guide you to propose solutions that align with both your interests and the company's. Being aware of emotional cues during these conversations can also provide deeper insights into what isn't being explicitly said, allowing you to tailor your responses and proposals effectively.

Another tactic is to explore and propose flexible working arrangements that might appeal to both parties. Offering to take on different roles or additional responsibilities without immediate pay raises can demonstrate your commitment and make a strong case for future discussions when the economic situation improves. These tactics also show your adaptability and willingness to contribute beyond traditional roles.

Develop an understanding of economic cycles and how they might affect the timing of salary negotiations. History shows that downturns are cyclical and often followed by periods of recovery. Timing your negotiation during signs of economic rebound, or aligning it with the company's financial cycle, can provide a more favorable context for your requests. Demonstrating an understanding of these cycles can build credibility and trust with your employer.

As you navigate these negotiations, consider also your own financial situation and risk tolerance. Economic downturns can be anxiety-inducing, especially if job security is threatened. Balance your immediate needs with long-term career goals. It's not just about surviving the present moment but positioning yourself for eventual upturns as well. Sometimes accepting a lower increase now can lead to greater opportunities later when conditions improve.

Finally, practice patience and remain resilient. Negotiations during economic hardships require persistence and sometimes entail several conversations. Keep the dialogue open and constructive, and maintain professional relationships, as these discussions can lay the groundwork for stronger connections and mutually beneficial outcomes in the future. Every negotiation during a downturn is a chance to demonstrate adaptability, foresight, and strategic thinking—skills that will be valuable throughout your career.

There's no one-size-fits-all strategy for managing negotiations during economic downturns, but by staying informed, flexible, and empathetic, you can navigate these conversations with confidence and clarity. Focus on outlining a path that not only supports your financial needs but also aligns with the company's future growth, ensuring mutual prosperity as the economy recovers.

Handling Counteroffers and Competing Offers

In the realm of salary negotiations, encountering counteroffers and competing offers is a unique but common situation. It presents both challenges and opportunities that require careful navigation to ensure a favorable outcome. When you've successfully attracted attention from more than one potential employer or prompted your current employer to reconsider their stance, you're placed in a powerful position.

However, it's essential to approach these scenarios with a strategic mindset.

First and foremost, it's crucial to understand what a counteroffer signifies. When an organization makes a counteroffer, it's an acknowledgment of your value. They are essentially expressing a desire to retain your skills by offering better terms. While this might inflate your ego temporarily, don't let it cloud your judgment about the initial reasons you considered leaving. Ensure these reasons aren't merely masked by temporary financial incentives, as dissatisfaction with work culture or lack of growth opportunities tend to re-emerge over time.

Competing offers from different employers unveil a different dynamic. In this case, you're valued by multiple parties, providing you with the leverage to negotiate from a position of strength. When you receive competing offers, consider evaluating them against your personal and professional priorities. This involves more than just comparing numbers. Think about factors such as work-life balance, potential for career growth, organizational culture, and alignment with your professional goals. A higher salary might seem appealing, but the overall work environment and growth opportunities are equally critical.

Once you've assessed the offers on the table, your next move is to tactfully communicate your decision. Clarity and honesty are paramount, especially if you're currently employed. When informing your current employer of a competing offer, be transparent about your reasons for considering the move. This isn't just courteous; it establishes a clear dialogue about your career aspirations and may open up discussions for better conditions within your current role.

It's also vital to consider timing and tactics when handling these situations. You're essentially managing a delicate balancing act between maintaining professional relationships and pursuing what's best for you. Don't be hasty. Take the time to deliberate on each offer's merits and drawbacks. If necessary, request additional time to consider the offers. This not only helps you make a well-considered decision but also communicates to the employers involved that you're thorough and committed to making a choice that's best for all parties involved.

One approach is to be forthright with companies about the existence of other offers, using them as leverage to potentially improve the terms provided. However, proceed with caution. Not all employers appreciate being pitted against another offer, and this could lead to burning bridges. Diplomacy, therefore, plays a significant role. Express gratitude for all offers received and refrain from adopting a transactional tone. This strategy, underpinned by respect and appreciation, is likely to yield more favorable outcomes.

Another insightful strategy lies in identifying your bottom line—understanding the minimum terms you're willing to accept. This forethought is critical when discussions intensify. Reflect on what constitutes a deal-breaker for you. Oftentimes, knowing your boundaries can provide the confidence needed to walk away from offers that don't align with your priorities, while also strengthening your position during negotiation.

Avoid making decisions based purely on emotional responses. Counteroffers and competing offers can be flattering, and it's easy to allow emotions to influence your judgment. Whether it's the newfound attention or the anxiety of deciding between impressive offers, maintain a rational perspective. Engaging in discussions with trusted advisors, mentors, or colleagues can provide insight beyond your immediate viewpoint and help ground your decisions in realistic terms.

Your decision should also take into account long-term career aspirations and how each offer aligns with these goals. Sometimes, a slightly lower salary in a company renowned for its career development programs and supportive culture can offer greater benefits in the long run than a high initial salary with limited growth prospects.

Lastly, when you've reached a decision, be gracious to those whose offers you decide not to accept. Express thanks and articulate that this was a difficult decision, ensuring that you leave doors open for potential future opportunities. It's not just about the deal at hand, but also about maintaining a professional reputation that speaks to your integrity and fair consideration.

Successfully managing counteroffers and competing offers involves a balance of strategic thought, clear communication, and emotional intelligence. Approaching these situations with a well-defined method will enhance your negotiating position today and set the tone for future interactions as you continue to build a rewarding career.

Chapter 22:
Case Studies in Successful Negotiations

Moving beyond theory to real-world applications, this chapter delves into pivotal case studies that illuminate the path to negotiation success. By examining diverse scenarios where individuals secured remarkable salary advances, readers will gain invaluable insights into the strategic maneuvers that drive successful outcomes. These stories bridge the gap between knowing what to do and seeing how it's done, illustrating how adaptable strategies can be tailored to fit unique negotiation landscapes. From leveraging research and timing to harnessing emotional intelligence and understanding cultural nuances, each case offers a blueprint for blending preparation with psychological insight. Whether it involves turning a tough "no" into a resounding "yes" or expertly negotiating the terms of a new position, these narratives are not only instructive but also inspire the confidence to reshape one's own negotiation journey.

Real-Life Success Stories

In the complex world of salary negotiations, real-life success stories not only inspire but also illuminate the path forward for others. These are tales of individuals who, against various odds, harnessed strategies and principles discussed throughout this book to secure significant salary enhancements. Let's explore some of these stories, examining the lessons they offer and why they matter to anyone looking to improve their negotiation outcomes.

Take Lucy, for instance, a mid-level marketing manager at a tech firm. For several years, Lucy had consistently outperformed her targets but felt overlooked during annual salary discussions. After immersing herself in negotiation strategies, Lucy came to realize her value in the industry was significantly higher than her current earnings. She meticulously researched market salaries and prepared a compelling case to present to her boss. Armed with confidence and evidence, Lucy approached her employer and articulated her accomplishments and market worth. Her preparedness and assertiveness paid off, resulting in a 20% salary increase. Lucy's story exemplifies the power of thorough preparation and self-advocacy.

In another compelling case, we have Jake, a software developer in a startup. Jake believed he was underpaid compared to his peers but thought the growing company couldn't afford to pay more. Instead of accepting defeat, Jake utilized a strategic approach. He highlighted his contributions and the losses the company could face without his expertise. During negotiations, he showcased potential future projects he could lead to drive growth. Instead of just asking for more money, Jake suggested a salary increase tied to achieving specific milestones, aligning his goals with the company's growth. This approach not only earned him a raise but also solidified his role as a key player in the company's future.

Then there's Maria, an accomplished writer who was stepping into the world of freelance. Transitioning from a salaried position, she was initially overwhelmed by the prospect of setting her rates and negotiating contracts. Through a network of fellow freelancers and mentors, Maria learned the importance of setting a strong anchor with her initial rate and the art of stacking value through her deliverables. She crafted proposals that highlighted not only her writing but also included social media promotion and keyword research services. This strategic bundling allowed Maria to secure contracts at rates much higher than when she priced each service individually.

A powerful example of negotiation during challenging economic times is Mark's story. Working in hospitality, a sector severely hit by the economic downturn, Mark's hours were cut, and he faced financial uncertainty. Instead of passively accepting the situation, Mark leveraged the skills he had developed over his years in hospitality management. He proposed a flexible work arrangement and took on projects to optimize operations, demonstrating cost savings to the company. By pivoting his role and proving his value in a new way, Mark not only preserved his position but also negotiated a performance-based bonus structure that incentivized savings and productivity.

Becky's journey is another testament to effective negotiation, encapsulating strategies tailored to a global context. Working in an international NGO, Becky faced a daunting negotiation across borders with her headquarters located thousands of miles away. She took time to understand cultural nuances and adjusted her communication style accordingly. Becky successfully communicated her achievements and future goals, using video conferences to maintain a personal connection with decision-makers. By framing her negotiation around mutual benefits and organizational values, she secured her desired salary increase along with added vacation days, showcasing how understanding and adapting to cultural contexts can greatly influence negotiation outcomes.

Finally, let's look at Sam, whose story is an exemplar of career progression through strategic salary negotiations. Starting as an entry-level analyst, Sam had a clear vision for his career path. At every opportunity for performance reviews, Sam didn't just ask for a raise. Instead, he had long-term discussions about his role, the value he added, and his career aspirations. He framed each discussion in terms of mutual growth, aligning his raises with responsibilities and long-term contributions to the company's objectives. Over a decade, Sam transitioned from entry-level to executive leadership, with salary increases that reflected not only his growing responsibilities but also his ability to continually demonstrate his evolving value.

These stories of Lucy, Jake, Maria, Mark, Becky, and Sam aren't mere anecdotes but are blueprints, reinforcing the principles and techniques that lead to successful salary negotiations. They remind us of the importance of preparation, adaptability, strategic thinking, and the ability to articulate one's value effectively. Real-life negotiations are complex, laden with personal and professional nuances, yet the underlying threads of strategy and communication remain integral to success.

As you reflect on these narratives, consider how the lessons learned by these individuals can inform your own negotiation strategies. Whether you're seeking a raise, stepping into freelance roles, or navigating a culturally diverse environment, the common thread is the confidence borne from preparation and the articulation of value. Let these stories be more than just tales; let them be catalysts that inspire and inform your next negotiation as you strive to achieve the pay and recognition you deserve.

Analyzing Different Negotiation Approaches

In the realm of salary negotiations, success often hinges on the approach you choose to take. Just like there isn't a one-size-fits-all solution for every professional challenge, negotiation tactics can vary greatly based on context, personality, and goals. Exploring various approaches provides insight into the art and science of negotiation, offering actionable strategies to improve outcomes at the negotiation table.

One approach that often garners success is the "interest-based" negotiation strategy. Unlike traditional adversarial bargaining, interest-based negotiation centers on understanding the underlying needs and concerns of both parties involved. This method emphasizes collaboration and mutual benefit rather than competition. Instead of viewing negotiations as a battlefield where one emerges victorious, this approach sees it as a problem-solving exercise where both sides come away satisfied. The result is often a more amicable agreement, strengthening professional relationships in the process.

For instance, I'm reminded of a recent case where a mid-level manager successfully negotiated a salary bump with a focus on shared interests. Rather than solely demanding a higher paycheck, she highlighted how aligning her compensation with industry standards could benefit both the company and herself. By tying her ask to potential outcomes like improved performance and long-term loyalty, she positioned herself as a collaborator rather than a competitor.

Another effective strategy is the "principled" negotiation approach, made famous by the book "Getting to Yes." This method insists on negotiating on the merits of the issues rather than through positional bargaining. It focuses on four key points: separating the people from the problem, focusing on interests not positions, generating options for mutual gain, and using objective criteria to make decisions. By adhering to these principles, negotiators can avoid unnecessary conflict and reach more sustainable agreements.

Take, for example, an IT specialist negotiating for a better benefits package. By applying principled negotiation tactics, he was able to outline objective industry trends that supported his request, effectively removing emotion from the conversation. By presenting data on competitor benefits and employee retention statistics, he successfully persuaded management to adjust the benefits, proving that well-substantiated facts can often speak louder than raw demands.

Furthermore, let's consider the "BATNA" concept within negotiations, or the Best Alternative to a Negotiated Agreement. Understanding one's BATNA is pivotal in negotiations because it gives you leverage and a fallback plan if talks stall. If your counterpart knows you have a strong BATNA, they are more likely to offer favorable terms to prevent you from walking away. Professionals adept at negotiating often prepare their BATNA thoroughly to ensure they're in a strong position.

Recently, a senior editor negotiating a job offer utilized a strong BATNA to her advantage. With a solid offer already in hand from another publisher, she was able to negotiate not only a higher salary but also flexible working conditions and enhanced creative control in the new role. Her clarity on what she'd do if negotiations failed gave her the confidence to stand firm on her requirements.

Another tactical approach is leveraging negotiation "anchoring." This psychological principle refers to the human tendency to rely heavily on the first piece of information encountered (the "anchor") when making decisions. In salary negotiations, the initial figure put forth can heavily influence the final agreement. By strategically setting the anchor, negotiators can frame the discussion in a way that benefits them.

Consider a software engineer who anchors the conversation with a slightly higher-than-expected salary proposal. This anchors the negotiation upwards, subtly suggesting the value she brings to the company. As a result, even if the employer counters with a lower offer, the final number often ends up higher than it would have been had she started with a lower figure.

Yet, it's essential to recognize that not all negotiation approaches will work in every situation. Cultural and organizational contexts can dictate the appropriateness and perceived aggressiveness of certain tactics. What works in a Fortune 500 boardroom might not be as effective in a nonprofit organization or a startup's informal setting. Understanding your environment, and tailoring your approach accordingly, is crucial.

For those negotiating in a cross-cultural context, the adaptation of strategies is even more important. In cultures where assertiveness may be seen as aggressiveness, a more collaborative or relationship-oriented approach may yield better results. Here, the ability to adapt not just tactics but mindset is key to successful outcomes.

The diverse landscape of negotiation techniques offers a wealth of possibilities. Whether it's through interest-based strategies, principled tactics, leveraging BATNAs, or effectively anchoring discussions, different approaches can provide pathways to success that align with individual goals and contexts. Honing these approaches involves practice, feedback, and a willingness to learn from every negotiation encounter.

Ultimately, there's no magic formula for successful negotiation, but exploring various strategies equips professionals with the tools they need to tailor their approach to each unique negotiation scenario. With practice and flexibility, anyone can evolve into a skilled negotiator, capable of navigating the complexities of salary discussions to achieve the compensation they deserve.

Chapter 23:
Continuous Improvement

In the ever-evolving landscape of salary negotiations, continuous improvement is your key to sustained success and growth. It's about embracing a mindset that leverages every negotiation—whether won or lost—as a valuable learning experience. Reflecting on past negotiations helps you pinpoint what strategies worked, what didn't, and how you can refine your approach for future encounters. This process of self-assessment allows you to build a personalized development plan, focusing on enhancing your strengths and addressing your weaknesses. By committing to this cycle of learning and adaptation, you position yourself to navigate future negotiations with increased confidence and competence. Remember, it's not just about negotiating better today, but about cultivating skills that will empower you throughout your career journey.

Learning from Past Negotiations

In the pursuit of mastering salary negotiations, it's crucial to understand that every negotiation is a learning experience. No matter the outcome, each encounter provides insights into what strategies work, what pitfalls to avoid, and how one's approach can be refined. The key to continuous improvement in this field lies in a constant and deliberate reflection on past negotiations. This isn't just an academic exercise; it's a practical strategy for future success.

The first step in learning from past negotiations is to honestly assess your performance. After a negotiation, it's tempting to quickly move on to the next challenge, especially if the result was not as hoped. However, taking the time to evaluate what happened is invaluable. Consider the objectives set before the negotiation and measure them against the results achieved. Were you clear and assertive in your requests? Did you adequately understand and navigate the employer's responses? By dissecting specific aspects of the negotiation, you can identify both strengths to build upon and weaknesses to address.

Another important aspect is understanding the emotional dynamics of your past negotiations. Emotions like anxiety or overconfidence can significantly influence outcomes. Reflecting on how these emotions played out in previous negotiations can offer lessons on how to better manage them in future encounters. Strategies such as mindfulness or stress management techniques can then be integrated into your preparation routine.

Feedback is another crucial component of learning. While it may seem awkward, asking for feedback from colleagues, mentors, or even the counterpart you negotiated with can offer perspectives you might not have considered. A mentor might notice, for example, that your body language seemed defensive, or that your tone shifted when discussing certain topics. External observations can illuminate blind spots in your negotiation approach, making them invaluable for growth.

Documenting each negotiation is also paramount. Maintaining a negotiation journal helps keep track of details that might be forgotten over time. Write down the strategies employed, the responses received, what felt good, and what didn't. Over time, patterns may emerge revealing what strategies consistently yield positive results and which ones require tweaking.

The importance of practicing self-compassion cannot be overstated when evaluating past negotiations. It's easy to fall into the trap of self-criticism, especially if negotiations didn't yield the desired outcome. Yet, being kind to oneself while acknowledging areas for improvement fosters a mindset conducive to growth. Recognizing that imperfection is part of the learning process encourages persistence and resilience, crucial traits for successful negotiators.

Another angle to consider is learning from successful negotiation models and case studies. By analyzing others' experiences and outcomes, you can glean strategies and techniques that are effective. Whether it's reading about a high-profile negotiation or attending a workshop, outside examples can provide valuable context and innovation to your approach.

To further enhance learning, consider setting specific, measurable goals for each future negotiation. Clear objectives not only provide direction but also offer benchmarks to assess progress after each engagement. Questions like, "Did I successfully articulate my value?" or "Was I able to counter lowball offers effectively?" can serve as gauges for assessing success and areas needing improvement.

Additionally, role-playing past negotiations with a trusted companion can provide a different perspective on how scenarios might have unfolded with different approaches. Role play adds an experiential component to reflection, enabling you to practice verbalizing strategies and receiving real-time feedback in a low-stakes environment, sharpening your skills for actual negotiations.

Finally, innovation and adaptability should underpin your learning process. The landscape of salary negotiation often shifts with changes in economic conditions, industry practices, and technological advancements. Your learning, hence, shouldn't just be reactive but also proactive, anticipating and experimenting with new strategies as these changes occur. Staying informed through reading, networking, and continuous education empowers you to stay ahead.

In summary, learning from past negotiations is about cultivating a cycle of continuous improvement, where each experience informs and enriches the next. By systematically evaluating past performances, actively seeking feedback, and embracing a mindset of growth and resilience, you can transform each negotiation into a stepping stone towards more successful and strategic salary discussions in the future. As you hone these skills, you're not just negotiating better salaries; you're fostering a powerful toolset that enhances your career trajectory.

Building a Personal Development Plan

Continuous improvement isn't just a concept; it's a commitment to growth that can significantly enhance your salary negotiation skills. At the core of this journey towards improvement lies a well-crafted personal development plan. This plan isn't merely a checklist of tasks but a dynamic roadmap guiding you towards becoming more adept in negotiations. Crafting a personal development plan involves assessing where you are, determining where you want to be, and laying out the steps to get there. It's a process that demands introspection, honesty, and a clear vision.

Begin by conducting a self-assessment to identify your current negotiation skills. This assessment isn't about critiquing yourself harshly but rather understanding the strengths and weaknesses you possess. It can be helpful to reflect on past negotiation experiences, paying close attention to what worked and what didn't. Were there moments when your confidence faltered, or times when your strategic approach was spot on? By acknowledging these instances, you can pinpoint the areas that require enhancement.

Once you have a grasp of your current abilities, it's time to set clear, achievable goals. These goals should be specific, measurable, attainable, relevant, and time-bound—often referred to as SMART goals. For instance, you might aim to improve your verbal communication skills by committing to joining a public speaking club within the next six months. Or, you could set a goal to familiarize yourself with cultural negotiation differences in anticipation of a meeting with an international client. Each goal should align with your ultimate aim of mastering salary negotiation.

Next, consider the resources and support systems you'll need to achieve these goals. Personal development doesn't occur in isolation. Books, workshops, online courses, and mentor relationships can all serve as excellent resources. Engaging with literature on negotiation techniques and psychological strategies can provide valuable insights. Likewise, attending workshops offers opportunities to practice negotiation scenarios in a safe environment, where feedback is constructive and immediate.

Incorporating feedback is a crucial element of any personal development plan. Seek out people who can provide you with honest, constructive criticism. This could be colleagues, mentors, or even peers who are fellow learners. Their perspectives can shed light on blind spots in your approach and offer suggestions you might not have considered. Remember, the goal of feedback is not to criticize but to foster growth and development.

As you work through your plan, it's important to track your progress. Regularly reviewing your goals and assessing your progress helps to keep you on track and allows you to make adjustments as needed. Be flexible and willing to recalibrate your goals based on what you learn and the challenges you encounter. Progress might be slow at times, and that's okay; what matters is the ongoing commitment to improvement.

In addition to skills and strategies, emotional intelligence plays a pivotal role in negotiations. Incorporating it into your plan can enhance your ability to read and respond to the emotions of others effectively. Developing emotional intelligence involves self-awareness, self-regulation, motivation, empathy, and social skills. Strengthening these areas can lead to more effective communication and better outcomes in negotiations.

Another vital component of a personal development plan is setting aside time for reflection. This involves not only contemplating your recent experiences and how they align with your goals but also evaluating your emotional responses to successes and setbacks. Reflection fosters a deeper understanding of your motivations, which can enhance your ability to navigate difficult negotiation scenarios.

An often-overlooked aspect of developing a comprehensive plan is the importance of staying informed about industry trends and best practices in negotiation. As economic conditions and workplace norms evolve, so do the strategies needed to negotiate effectively. Devote time to staying abreast of changes in your field, which can be accomplished by reading industry publications, attending seminars, and participating in networking events.

Finally, understand that personal development is a lifelong process. As you achieve your goals and build new skill sets, continue to challenge yourself by setting new objectives. Avoid complacency by regularly seeking out new opportunities to learn and grow. By consistently pushing the boundaries of your knowledge and capabilities, you'll remain agile and prepared for a wide array of negotiation scenarios, ultimately elevating your negotiation skill to a formidable level.

Building a personal development plan for salary negotiation is not a task to be taken lightly. However, with dedication and the right approach, it can lead to significant personal and professional growth.

Embrace the process with a spirit of curiosity and persistence, and the rewards will come in the form of greater confidence, improved negotiation outcomes, and a career trajectory aligned with your aspirations.

Chapter 24:
Practicing Negotiation Skills

Practicing negotiation skills transforms theoretical knowledge into practical prowess. It's not just about learning the techniques, but ingraining them through repeated, real-world simulations. Picture it like training for a marathon; the more mock negotiations you engage in, the more natural and effective your responses become. During these practice sessions, pay close attention to evaluating and refining your techniques, embracing feedback as a powerful tool for growth. Whether you're role-playing with a mentor or participating in an online negotiation workshop, each scenario offers a unique learning opportunity. By constantly practicing, you become adept at navigating complex interactions and develop a keen sense of timing and strategy. This consistent preparation builds confidence, ensuring that when it comes time to negotiate for real, you're armed with the skills needed to articulate your worth and achieve the salary you deserve.

Engaging in Mock Negotiations

When it comes to mastering the art of salary negotiation, practice isn't just essential; it's transformative. Engaging in mock negotiations provides an invaluable opportunity to rehearse your skills in a risk-free environment. Consider it a rehearsal before the main performance, where you can experiment, make mistakes, and refine your approach without the pressure of real stakes. For many, the thought of negotiating a salary can stir up anxiety and uncertainty, but mock negotiations help demystify the process and instill a deep sense of confidence.

In a mock negotiation, you're essentially putting yourself in a simulation of what real-world negotiations might entail. This active learning strategy allows you to experiment with different techniques and observe their outcomes without the worry of any negative consequences. Whether it's with a friend, a colleague, or a professional coach, this practice hones your ability to think on your feet and adapt to different scenarios. The more you engage in these exercises, the more you build a natural and instinctive negotiation muscle that will serve you well in actual salary discussions.

One of the primary benefits of mock negotiations is that they offer a safe space to face and address personal barriers. Are you prone to freezing up when asked tough questions? Do you find it difficult to assert your worth? Participating in mock sessions can bring these issues to light. It's not uncommon to experience a range of emotions during a negotiation—everything from nervousness to excitement. Practicing in a controlled setting allows you to become familiar with your emotional responses and learn how to manage them effectively.

Another crucial aspect of mock negotiations is the opportunity they provide for feedback. After a session, sit down with the person you practiced with and dissect what went well and what could be improved. Effective feedback is constructive and specific; it should focus on the nuances of your communication style, your body language, and the substance of your arguments. Receiving and acting on feedback helps refine your approach, transforming what was once a mediocre performance into a compelling and polished act.

Mock negotiations are not just about bettering your negotiation skills but also about gaining insight into the negotiation process as a whole. They give you the chance to see things from the other side of the table. Consider taking turns playing the role of the employer or the hiring manager in practice sessions. By understanding the perspective and priorities of your counterpart, you can tailor your strategy more effectively. This experience helps build empathy and sharpens your ability to anticipate the arguments and tactics the other party might use.

To make your mock negotiation sessions more effective, strive to make them as realistic as possible. Gather information about typical salary ranges and benefits packages within your field. Prepare a script or a list of key points you want to cover, but also leave room for improvisation based on how the negotiation unfolds. Use real-world scenarios that you might encounter, such as discussing a raise with a current employer or bargaining for a better starting package in a new job. The closer your mock negotiation resembles reality, the more confident and prepared you will feel when it's time for the real deal.

While engaging in mock negotiations, pay close attention to both verbal and non-verbal communication cues. A significant portion of negotiation is about reading the room—interpreting changes in tone, body language, and the pacing of the conversation. Practicing these skills helps enhance your ability to pick up on subtle cues that indicate when you might need to pivot your approach or delve deeper into a particular point. This can be the difference between a favorable outcome and a missed opportunity.

Mock negotiations also encourage strategic thinking. As you practice, consider various strategies and tactics and how they might play out. For instance, you might experiment with using silence to your advantage, allowing the other party to fill in the gaps, which can often lead to them making concessions. Or, you might try out the anchoring technique, where you start with a higher salary figure to set a favorable reference point for subsequent discussions. The possibilities are vast, and practice is where you can see first-hand what works best for you.

In addition to practicing negotiation tactics, mock negotiations provide a platform for honing your listening skills. Active listening is a crucial element of successful negotiations, as it not only shows respect and attentiveness but also provides you with critical information that can inform your strategy. Often, what is said between the lines can be just as important as the points explicitly stated. By practicing active listening in mock sessions, you enhance your ability to pick up on cues that can be leveraged to your advantage when negotiating for real.

It's worth noting that mock negotiations are not a one-time exercise. Like any skill, negotiation requires continuous practice and refinement. As you progress in your career and face new challenges, the context of your negotiations will evolve, necessitating an ongoing commitment to practice and self-improvement. Each mock session builds on the previous one, allowing for incremental advances in your skills, understanding, and confidence.

Ultimately, mock negotiations are about preparation and empowerment. They're your ticket to becoming a more assertive and articulate negotiator, capable of navigating the complexities of salary discussions with poise and purpose. By investing time into these practice sessions, you're equipping yourself with the tools needed to walk into any negotiation scenario ready to secure the compensation you deserve.

So, take the plunge and incorporate mock negotiations into your regular preparation routine. Challenge yourself to push beyond your comfort zone and embrace the learning curve. With determination and practice, you'll find yourself not only becoming a proficient negotiator but also empowering yourself to seize the opportunities and rewards that come your way.

Evaluating and Refining Techniques

Mastering negotiation skills is akin to honing an art form; it demands constant evaluation and refinement. As you delve into practicing negotiation skills, the importance of a reflective approach becomes paramount. Each negotiation encounter presents a unique opportunity to learn and grow. By assessing your techniques critically, you can pinpoint areas that require improvement and identify strategies that worked well.

One pivotal aspect of evaluating negotiation techniques is maintaining a negotiation journal. Document the context, strategies deployed, and outcomes of each negotiation experience. This practice serves as a valuable reference, helping you track progress over time. Analyzing past negotiations offers insight into patterns of success and areas that may need adjustment. This reflection allows you to develop a deeper understanding of your negotiation style and adjust your approach as necessary.

Feedback, both self-reflected and external, is instrumental in refining your skills. Seeking feedback from colleagues or mentors post-negotiation can provide an objective perspective. Their insights may uncover blind spots you hadn't noticed, aiding in a more comprehensive evaluation of your performance. Equally important is self-assessment. After each negotiation, ask yourself questions: Were my objectives clear? Did I listen actively? How did I handle counteroffers? This introspection can reveal areas for growth.

Role-playing sessions offer another powerful method for refining negotiation techniques. They simulate real-world scenarios under controlled conditions, allowing you to practice and refine skills without the pressure of actual stakes. These sessions can be tailored to focus on specific areas of improvement, whether it's handling difficult conversations, employing persuasive techniques, or articulating value propositions effectively. Constructive feedback during role-playing exercises provides actionable insights into your negotiation approach.

Moreover, analyzing body language is an often-overlooked yet crucial aspect of negotiation. Body language can convey confidence or insecurity and can significantly influence the outcome of negotiations. Video recording your role-play sessions can be enlightening. Watching yourself can highlight subconscious habits that may undermine your verbal communications. Are you maintaining good eye contact? Does your posture exude confidence? Such reflections can help you align your non-verbal cues with your verbal messages for a more cohesive presentation.

Incorporating learnings from psychological principles can refine your approach further. For instance, understanding and leveraging the anchoring effect can help you set a favorable starting point in negotiations. You can track how effectively you've applied these principles by reviewing your negotiation records. Did the anchoring approach help settle on favorable terms? Adjust and refine your use of psychological leverage points to see what works best in different contexts.

It's also vital to periodically assess your negotiation toolkit. Are there techniques you haven't explored yet? As the professional landscape evolves, so too should your skill set. Consider adding new techniques to your repertoire. Explore various negotiation styles, like competing, collaborating, or compromising, in different situations to see which yields the best outcomes. Expanding your toolkit equips you better to handle diverse negotiation scenarios effectively.

Evaluating techniques also involves measuring tangible outcomes. This means setting clear, measurable goals before negotiations and assessing results against these benchmarks. Did you achieve the salary increase you were aiming for? If not, analyze what held you back. Was it the strategy, timing, or external factors? By understanding how different elements contribute to outcomes, you can refine your future strategies to be more effective.

Commit to continuous learning by staying informed on negotiation trends and developments. Workshops, webinars, and professional courses can introduce new strategies and perspectives, enriching your negotiation acumen. The negotiation field doesn't stand still, and neither should your learning efforts. Engaging with current literature and thought leaders in the negotiation space keeps your techniques sharp and relevant.

Ultimately, refining negotiation techniques is a dynamic, ongoing journey. It's about embracing trial and error, learning from successes and setbacks, and remaining adaptable in the face of changing circumstances. By continuously evaluating and refining your skills, you build a strong foundation for successful salary negotiations that align with your professional goals and aspirations.

Chapter 25:
Building a Support Network

Building a support network is a vital step in mastering the art of salary negotiation. Whether you're angling for a raise or securing the best starting salary in a new position, having a solid base of allies is your secret weapon. Mentors and trusted colleagues can offer guidance and feedback, helping you refine your strategies and bolster your confidence. Cultivating relationships within your industry not only opens doors to new opportunities but also arms you with the insights needed to effectively articulate your value. Actively engaging with professional networks allows you to tap into shared experiences and learn from others' victories and setbacks. By surrounding yourself with those who genuinely want to see you thrive, you empower yourself to navigate negotiations with skill and poise, amplifying your potential to achieve your financial goals. This interconnected web of support becomes your safety net and springboard, reminding you that you're not alone—and that success is a collaborative journey.

Identifying Mentors and Allies

Building a successful career, especially when it comes to negotiating salaries, isn't just about mastering techniques and understanding the market. It's also about having a robust support network. At the heart of this network are mentors and allies who can offer guidance, share experiences, and provide opportunities that can be pivotal to your negotiation success.

Identifying the right mentors often starts with recognizing individuals who exemplify the traits and paths you aspire to. These are people who have navigated similar challenges and can provide not just support, but insider insights that elevate your negotiating acumen. Seeking out mentors doesn't mean finding someone who is perfect or has all the answers, but rather someone who can offer a veteran perspective and who resonates with your professional aspirations.

Allies, on the other hand, are often peers or colleagues who are on similar journeys. They might share your commitments to personal and professional growth or have faced similar hurdles in their career paths. Allies are valuable because they can offer real-time feedback and share resources in a way that only those traveling a parallel path can provide. Finding such allies is invaluable, as they offer collective strength and often, a more diversified perspective than a single mentor might offer.

An essential step in identifying these mentors and allies is through active participation in professional communities, whether they're industry-specific organizations, online forums, or social media groups. These spaces often host individuals who are naturally inclined to share knowledge and foster connections. Regularly contributing to these communities can naturally lead to the formation of valuable relationships.

A mentor's guidance can have a transformative impact on your salary negotiation skills. They can help frame your mindset, influence the way you perceive value, and guide your preparation strategies. A mentor who understands the nuances of the job market and who has navigated difficult negotiations can provide narratives and strategies that are not found in textbooks. Their real-world experiences can demystify the negotiation process, allowing you to approach situations with both confidence and insight.

Building a network of mentors and allies isn't always instantaneous. It requires authenticity, patience, and a willingness to reciprocate. When engaging with potential mentors or allies, it's crucial to approach these relationships with sincerity and a clear idea of what you hope to learn or achieve. It's also important to consider what you can offer in return, establishing a mutually beneficial relationship that thrives on mutual respect and shared goals.

A great way to cement these relationships is by reaching out regularly, whether it's through emails, social media, or in-person meet-ups. Sharing achievements and expressing gratitude can go a long way in maintaining these connections. Similarly, discussing any challenges you're facing can lead to constructive feedback that might offer a new perspective or solution you hadn't considered.

Moreover, you should not underestimate the power of learning from peers. While mentors often have more experience, peers can offer solidarity and share contemporary insights into industry trends, role expectations, and emergent negotiation strategies that might not have filtered through to more senior levels yet. Engaging in these conversations offers a dynamic learning environment where ideas can be challenged and refined.

Another aspect of building these relationships is the serendipity factor. Sometimes, informal gatherings, webinars, or industry conferences serve as fertile grounds for meeting future mentors or allies. Being open to these opportunities and ready to engage meaningfully can turn a chance conversation into a long-term, career-boosting relationship.

The encouragement and support from mentors and allies can significantly impact your self-belief and negotiation outcomes. They serve as a sounding board for your ideas, encouraging you when doubts creep in and mentoring you through the complexities of multi-step negotiation processes. Allies can bolster your resolve by offering first-hand testimony of what can be achieved, serving as real-world proof of the possibilities that lie ahead.

In summary, identifying mentors and allies is a pivotal component of building a support network that'll enhance your salary negotiation skills. These relationships offer both tactical advice and emotional encouragement. The guidance these individuals provide often goes beyond mere negotiation skills, encompassing personal growth, career trajectory, and broadening one's understanding of workplace dynamics.

By actively seeking out and nurturing these relationships, you'll be better equipped to not just navigate negotiations, but to thrive in your career overall. The collective wisdom and support of mentors and allies create a foundation that empowers you to stand firm, articulate your worth, and achieve what you deserve. As you embark on this journey, remember that these connections are a cornerstone of your personal and professional development, leading you to success in salary negotiations and beyond.

Networking for Career Advancement

Networking can be a powerful tool in the arsenal of anyone looking to enhance their career prospects, particularly when it comes to salary negotiations. Building a supportive and strategic network doesn't just open doors—it's an accelerator for career advancement. In the context of negotiation, networking is not merely about the people you know but about nurturing relationships that bring mutual benefits. Through this exchange of value, a well-connected network can offer insights, opportunities, and leverage that can significantly impact your earnings.

Just imagine starting a negotiation already armed with insights gleaned from your network about the company's ethos or compensation practices. This is where networking shines. Friends, colleagues, and mentors provide inside knowledge that a job listing or online research just won't give you. When you have access to firsthand information, your confidence takes a leap, and that confidence is palpable when you walk into negotiation rooms.

Networking isn't about random interactions; it's intentional and strategic. Begin by identifying key people in your industry. Attend seminars, join professional groups, and leverage platforms like LinkedIn to connect with others who may offer valuable insights into your field. But remember, it's not only about reaching out to those at the top of the ladder. Often, peers or those just a rung above you have faced similar challenges and can offer practical advice. Everyone's experience holds potential value.

Your network is also a reflection of your personal brand. Building a strong, consistent, and authentic presence in your industry can draw people toward you, transforming connections into an opportunity for career growth. Sharing your own insights and showing genuine interest in others' success stories not only enriches your network but positions you as a valuable component within it. This reciprocal approach ensures that relationships are not one-sided but are sources of ongoing collaboration and growth.

It's crucial to maintain these relationships over time. Stay in touch and show interest in your contacts' endeavors, not only when you need something. Engaging regularly with your network will make seeking help during your salary negotiation far less daunting. When people see you as an active participant in their professional circles, they're more likely to offer help without a second thought. Establishing credibility in your network is an investment that yields dividends when it counts.

If you're unsure where to start, consider seeking out a mentor. Mentors provide guidance, resources, and sometimes, even introductions that might be pivotal in securing a better financial package. In negotiations, these seasoned individuals can provide unique strategies or highlight potential pitfalls you may not have considered. Their experiences in similar scenarios are invaluable, often acting as a mirror to reflect what's possible.

The art of negotiation also benefits from observing and learning from those around you. Attend industry events where seasoned negotiators share their expertise and strategies. These events are prime opportunities not only to learn but also to introduce yourself and expand your network. By engaging with experts and thought leaders, you're positioning yourself to receive wisdom that can't be gleaned from books or online articles alone.

In terms of psychological tools, networking provides what's known as "social proof," a powerful driver in salary negotiations. Companies often see individuals with strong networks as more valuable, perceiving them as industry influencers or insiders. This perceived value can sway salary discussions in your favor, as employers recognize the inherent benefits of hiring someone who comes with a network of resources and industry insights.

Additionally, consider how collaboration and partnerships within your network can directly affect your work performance, leading to justifiable reasons for a pay raise. When you collaborate with skilled individuals, it enhances the quality of your contributions, making you more indispensable to your employer. This, in turn, sets a solid foundation for your negotiation talks since you're not only presenting your own achievements but also the added value of your collaborative efforts.

Yet, as you engage with your network, it's vital to remember this isn't about transactional relationships. Instead, focus on the genuine value you can offer others. Whether it's sharing a resource, offering to introduce two people, or providing feedback, these small actions build goodwill. Over time, they'll circle back to benefit your own career aspirations, especially during salary negotiations where endorsements and references might play crucial roles.

Lastly, be mindful that the most powerful networks are built on diversity. Diversify your connections across industries, cultures, and experiences. This variety enriches your knowledge base and presents unexpected opportunities for learning and growth. A diverse network is more adaptable and better equipped to provide fresh perspectives that might transform your approach to negotiation and career progression altogether.

Through consistent effort and strategic engagement, your network becomes a fundamental support system as you navigate your career. Not only can it help you secure a favorable salary, but it also sustains your long-term growth and development. By investing the right resources into networking, you are, in effect, carving out a path to career advancement that is both supportive and dynamic.

Conclusion

As we reach the end of our exploration into the art and science of salary negotiation, it's important to reflect on the journey we've taken through these pages. We've traversed the psychological landscape that shapes our financial decisions and ventured into the depths of negotiation tactics. We've examined the subtleties of communication, both verbal and non-verbal, and have outlined strategies for every conceivable scenario and challenge in the negotiation room. Now, it's time to bring it all together and focus on how these insights can empower you to navigate your own path to financial success and fulfillment.

Salary negotiation isn't a mere transactional process; it's deeply rooted in understanding your worth and effectively communicating that to others. It requires a blend of introspection, research, and strategic planning coupled with emotional intelligence and eloquent expression. Recognizing the mindset and emotional barricades that often thwart our progress is a critical step toward overcoming them.

The skills and techniques discussed in this book are not just academic exercises; they are actionable tools intended to boost your confidence and decision-making abilities in real-world situations. Whether you're seeking a raise in your current job, negotiating the terms of a new role, or trying to secure a better deal as a freelancer, these foundational principles are your guide.

One of the most empowering aspects of salary negotiation is the ability to set realistic goals and map out a strategic approach to achieving them. This involves investing time and effort into researching market values, understanding the nuances of timing, and crafting a compelling narrative around your abilities and contributions.

Effective negotiation also hinges on the psychology of persuasion. By leveraging principles like anchoring and reciprocity, you can gain the upper hand while maintaining professional decorum. It's a delicate balance of assertiveness and empathy that can yield favorable outcomes without damaging relationships.

Let's not forget the role of flexibility and resilience throughout the negotiation process. Sometimes, negotiations don't result in the immediate outcome we desire, but handling rejections gracefully and converting them into learning opportunities can be just as rewarding. Mastering the art of turning a "no" into constructive feedback or a future possibility is an invaluable skill.

Moreover, navigating the complexities of gender and cultural considerations has never been more pertinent than in today's workplace environment. Empowering yourself with knowledge about these dynamics can enable you to advocate effectively, not just for yourself but for others who might face similar challenges.

This book encourages you to embrace a mindset of continuous improvement. Rehearsing negotiation scenarios, learning from past experiences, and actively seeking feedback are essential practices for honing your craft. As with any other skill, negotiation requires practice, patience, and persistence. It's about building a repertoire of techniques and adapting them to fit unique situations and personal styles.

Also, the potential of technology in streamlining preparation and facilitating remote negotiations can't be overstated. In a world where virtual interactions have become the norm, having a command of technological tools can significantly enhance the negotiation experience, making it more effective and efficient.

Finally, the power of a supportive network cannot be underestimated. Building a group of mentors, allies, and like-minded individuals can provide you with insights, encouragement, and opportunities that would be difficult to achieve alone. It's about creating a community where mutual support propels everyone to greater heights.

In conclusion, consider this book a springboard to a more empowered and self-assured version of yourself. The key to mastering salary negotiation doesn't lie in a secret formula but in understanding the interplay of human psychology, cultural fluency, communication, and strategic planning. As you apply these principles and strategies, you will grow not only in your professional life but also in your confidence and ability to advocate for your value. May your journey henceforth be one of success, growth, and fearless negotiation. Your future is yours to negotiate—seize it with all the knowledge and skills you've gained.

Appendix A:
Appendix

As we conclude our exploration of salary negotiation strategies, this appendix serves as a supplementary resource to enhance your journey. It's designed to consolidate key learnings and offer practical insights that might not have been completely covered in the main chapters. Salary negotiations are more than just conversations about pay; they're opportunities to redefine your career trajectory, establish your worth, and gain financial empowerment.

Additional Resources for Negotiation

Consider seeking out further reading from experts in negotiation and behavioral psychology to deepen your understanding.

Engage in online workshops or courses that simulate real-life negotiation scenarios, offering a hands-on approach to skill enhancement.

Utilize negotiation role-playing apps that allow you to practice in a risk-free environment, honing your techniques and receiving instant feedback.

Books and Articles

Explore literature that intersects finance and psychology, helping you understand the underpinnings of negotiation dynamics.

Investigate articles focused on emerging trends in workplace negotiations, especially those dealing with remote and hybrid work settings.

Networking and Mentorship

Building a network of like-minded professionals can provide invaluable support and advice. Consider joining forums or groups where negotiation experiences are shared and discussed. Seek out mentors who have traversed the path and can offer personalized guidance in navigating complex negotiations.

Innovation in Negotiation Strategies

The negotiation landscape is continuously evolving with technological advancements and shifts in workplace culture. Staying updated with these changes can provide a significant edge. Experiment with employing AI tools or data analytics to prepare for negotiations, making your arguments more compelling and data-driven.

Reflection and Continuous Growth

The art of negotiation is not a one-time skill but a lifelong pursuit. Reflect on past negotiations to identify what strategies were successful and which areas need improvement. Develop a personal growth plan that includes periodic reassessment of your goals and skills, ensuring you remain prepared for future opportunities.

In summary, this appendix serves as a launchpad for further exploration and mastery in salary negotiations, empowering you to achieve the compensation and professional recognition you deserve. Continue building your capabilities, leverage available resources, and remain proactive in your pursuit of excellence.